MICR
~TIPS &

MICROWAVE
~ TIPS & TIMINGS ~

BRIDGET JONES

WARD LOCK LIMITED · LONDON

© Ward Lock 1989
© Illustrations Ward Lock 1989

First published in Great Britain in 1989
by Ward Lock Limited, 8 Clifford Street
London W1X 1RB, an Egmont Company

Designed by Cherry Randell
Text filmset/set in Sabon
by Columns of Reading
Printed and bound in Scotland
by William Collins & Co. Glasgow

British Library Cataloguing in Publication Data

Jones, Bridget
  Microwave tips and timings.
  1. Microwave ovens, – Manuals
  I. Title
  641.5'882

ISBN 0–7063–6812–6

The author and publishers would like to thank the
following for help with this book:
Nordic Ware (UK) Limited for providing a microwave
pressure cooker for testing; Siemens Domestic
Appliances and Toshiba (UK) Limited for providing
microwave cookers.

INTRODUCTION;
– USING THIS BOOK

Microwave Tips & Timings provides an invaluable A–Z guide to the details of microwave cooking. Information on the basic principles of using your microwave, the utensils and accessories to use and avoid, and the foods that can be cooked successfully in it is all given in alphabetical order. There are also notes on those foods which do not cook well in the microwave.

Under each food entry you will find basic information on how the item should be prepared and cooked, along with cooking times and any special instructions to ensure success. The Power Settings section (page 124) explains the different microwave wattages and clarifies any effect these may have on cooking times. A selection of specialities that are particularly well suited to this cooking method are also given under the relevant food entries, as well as favourite recipes, which are also listed in the recipe index on page 158. Sauces, accompaniments and serving suggestions are all given and cross-referenced, so you can flick to the advice you require immediately.

Bridget Jones trained as a home economist, before becoming a cookery editor and then a cookery writer. She has researched, tested and edited numerous recipes – a total of over 1000 in the microwave. A confirmed microwave user, she has distilled her time-saving tips and ideas for creating successful dishes and avoiding failures in this essential kitchen dictionary.

A-Z DICTIONARY OF MICROWAVE COOKING

A

ABSORBENT KITCHEN PAPER
When cooking foods which do not require covering with a lid but which may spatter, for example bacon rashers, then place a sheet of absorbent kitchen paper loosely over the top. Place absorbent paper under bread squares for croûtons (see page 59) or under herbs when drying them (see page 87), to absorb moisture.

ALMONDS
Flaked, slivered or split blanched almonds can be browned in the microwave either dry or with butter.
Dry Browned Almonds Place 50g/2oz almonds in a small basin. Cook on full for 2½–3½ minutes, rearranging the nuts halfway through. Use as a decoration for cakes and desserts, in salads or other savoury dishes.
Browned Almonds in Butter Place 50g/2oz almonds in a small basin with 50g/2oz butter and cook on full for 3–4 minutes, or until the nuts are lightly browned. Pour over cooked trout, chicken portions or vegetables before serving.

APPLES
Apples cook very well in the microwave, either whole or cut up. The fruit can be quartered and stewed until tender or cut up and cooked until reduced to a purée.
Defrosting Apple Slices Place the frozen apple slices in a covered dish. Cook on defrost setting for the

following times:

225g/8oz – 3–4 minutes	
450g/1lb – 6–7 minutes	

If the slices are frozen in a block it will need gently breaking during defrosting and about 2 minutes extra time, depending on how tightly packed the slices are.

Baked Apples Wash, dry and core the fruit (use medium-sized cooking apples), then score the skin with a knife all round the middle to prevent bursting. Place the apples as far apart as possible in a dish and fill their middles with sultanas or raisins, demerara sugar, a pinch of ground cinnamon and a few chopped walnuts. Alternative fillings include mincemeat or dried fruits flavoured with orange rind. Top each with a knob of butter and cook on full for the following times:

1 apple – 2–2½ minutes	
2 apples – 3½–4 minutes	
3 apples – 5–5½ minutes	
4 apples – 6–6½ minutes	

If you are cooking more than two whole apples rotate each one halfway through cooking.

Apple Purée Peel, core and slice 450g/1lb cooking apples and place in a dish with a sprinkling of lemon juice and 2 tablespoons water. Cover and cook on full for 5–7 minutes, stirring halfway through the cooking time. Beat well and press through a sieve if you like. Sweeten to taste.

Apple Sauce Peel, core and slice 450g/1lb cooking apples and place in a large basin or casserole dish with 100g/4oz sugar. Add a knob of butter, cover and cook on full for 6–8 minutes, or until the apples are very soft. Beat well until smooth and cool before serving.

Stewed Apples Mix 175g/6oz sugar, the juice of ½ lemon and 150ml/¼ pint water in a casserole dish. Add a strip of pared lemon rind and cook on full for 3–4 minutes, or until very hot, then stir well until the sugar has dissolved. Peel, core and quarter 4 medium cooking apples (about 675g/1½lb) and add them to the syrup, spooning it over the pieces of fruit. Cover and cook on full for 5–7 minutes, rearranging the apples halfway through cooking. The cooked apples should be just tender, not fallen, and still with a little bite. Serve hot with custard (see page 62) or cream. For a half quantity, allow 1½–2 minutes for dissolving the sugar and 3–4 minutes to soften the apples. The cooking time for both quantities depends on the type of apple – some cooking apples soften very quickly.

Toffee Apples Prepare a dark golden caramel (see page 33). Spear 4 small dessert apples on to wooden sticks and dip them into the hot caramel immediately it is cooked. Rotate the apples to coat them evenly, then place on greased greaseproof paper or waxed paper to cool. Eat on the same day as coating.

APRICOTS

Both fresh and dried apricots can be cooked in the microwave.

Baked Apricots Heat 100g/4oz sugar with 150ml/¼ pint water and the juice of ½ lemon on full for 3–4 minutes, until very hot, then stir until the sugar has dissolved. Halve 450g/1lb apricots and remove their stones. If you like, crack a few of the stones and add the kernels to the syrup. Toss the apricot halves in the syrup, cover and cook on full for about 5 minutes, or until the fruit is tender. Stir halfway through cooking.

Dried Apricots

> *When cooking in the microwave, dried apricots do not have to be pre-soaked.*

Place 225g/8oz apricots in a dish with about 300ml/½ pint water to cover the fruit. Cover the dish and cook on full for 15 minutes. Leave to stand for 10–15 minutes, then use as required.

Apricot Compote For a deliciously simple dessert, prepare the apricots as above, substituting sweet cider or wine for the water. Add a cinnamon stick and a little grated orange rind, and cook as above. Sweeten with a little sugar, honey or syrup to taste, then serve warm or well chilled with whipped cream or thick, Greek-style yogurt.

ARCING

This is the term used for the sparking which occurs if metal, or dishes decorated with metallic paint, are used in the microwave. Never operate the microwave empty as this will also cause sparking. If you see any sparking, then immediately switch off the microwave and check for the cause of the problem.

ARTICHOKES

Globe artichokes can be cooked with ease and speed in the microwave, and Jerusalem artichokes can be prepared to perfection.

Globe Artichokes Cut off the long thick stalks, snip off the leaf ends and remove any loose, very low set outer leaves. Wash thoroughly, then place in a large dish or roasting bag. Sprinkle with 2 tablespoons lemon juice and 2 tablespoons water. Cover or loosely close the bag with a microwave-proof tie or elastic band, allowing room for the steam to escape.

Cook on full for the following times:

1 artichoke – 6–8 minutes
2 artichokes – 9–11 minutes
3 artichokes – 12–14 minutes
4 artichokes – 15–18 minutes

The timing depends on the size of the artichokes and on their age and tenderness. Leave the cooked vegetables to stand, still in their cooking container, for about 5 minutes. Test to make sure they are tender by pulling off one of the outer leaves which should come away easily. Carefully remove the leaves from the centre and scrape out the hairy choke, then serve as required. They are good warm, with a well-flavoured oil and vinegar dressing, and fresh bread and butter.

Jerusalem Artichokes Peel or scrub 450g/1lb artichokes, removing any bruised bits. Place in a dish and add 2 tablespoons water and 1 tablespoon lemon juice. Mix well, cover and cook on full for 8–10 minutes, stirring halfway through cooking. Leave covered for 2–3 minutes before draining and serving. The cooked artichokes should be tender but not too soft. They are delicious topped with buttered almonds (see page 6) and snipped chives.

ASPARAGUS

Asparagus cooks well in the microwave, either fresh or frozen. Trim and peel the stems, then place the asparagus spears in a roasting bag. Add 2 tablespoons water and close the end of the bag loosely with a microwave-proof tie or elastic band, leaving room for the steam to escape. Cook on full for the following times:

225g/8oz – 4–6 minutes
450g/1lb – 7–9 minutes

Frozen asparagus does not take much longer than fresh but do not add water:

225g/8oz – 6–8 minutes
450g/1lb – 9–12 minutes

Drain and serve with melted butter poured over.

AUBERGINES
Whole, sliced or cubed, aubergines cook quickly in the microwave to give moist, tender results. Trim the ends off the vegetables, then prick them all over if they are to be cooked whole. Place whole aubergines on absorbent kitchen paper on a plate. Slices or cubes can be cooked in a covered dish or roasting bag; stir or rearrange halfway through cooking. For mashing into a dip (good flavoured with garlic and chopped spring onion, stirred with soured cream) or slicing and using in a moussaka, cook the vegetables whole; leave to cool slightly before slicing or cutting. The following guide to timing is for cooking on full:

1 medium	whole	3–4 minutes
2 medium	whole	5–6 minutes
450g/1lb	sliced or cubed, tossed in a little oil	8–10 minutes
675g/1½lb	sliced or cubed, tossed in a little oil	12–15 minutes

Aubergines with Tomato Cook 1 chopped onion and 1 crushed clove garlic in 3 tablespoons oil on full for 3 minutes, then mix with the sliced or cubed aubergines and cook as above. Season, sprinkle with chopped mint or parsley and a little peeled diced tomato before serving.

Tip *If slicing or cubing aubergines place in a colander, sprinkle well with salt and leave for at least 30 minutes, to drain off the bitter juices. Rinse and dry before cooking.*

AVOCADO

Avocado flesh heats very quickly in the microwave to make a delicious starter. The halved avocados can be heated and topped with soured cream and chives, cream cheese and crispy bacon bits (see page 14).

Plain white avocado dishes can be used to support the avocados as they are heated.

Sprinkle the cut surface with lemon juice, cook on full for the following times, then top and serve immediately they are cooked.

1 medium, halved – 1 minute
2 medium, halved – 2–2½ minutes

 **B**

BABY FOOD AND MILK

The microwave is particularly useful for warming a baby's bottle or a small dish of puréed food.

However, it is important to remember that the microwave warms milk to feeding temperature very quickly, and small amounts of puréed foods will also become very hot quickly.

Before heating milk, remove the teat from the bottle and replace the flat and screw-top lids. Allow about

15–30 seconds on full, shake the bottle to distribute the heat evenly and then test the temperature by sprinkling a few drops of milk on to the back of your hand.

Small amounts of puréed foods can be warmed in a plastic dish or small basin. Again, timing is very short and a 150ml/¼ pint portion, or one jar or a small can (transferred, of course), will need about 30–60 seconds on full. Check and stir the food after 30 seconds, then replace it in the microwave for a further 15 seconds before checking again. The time depends on the starting temperature of the food; always stir and taste the purée before feeding baby.

Small portions of frozen puréed foods can be defrosted and reheated in one operation. Place the frozen purée in a basin and allow 1–2 minutes on full for 150ml/¼ pint. Break up the purée as soon as it softens, then stir well and taste before feeding baby.

BACON
Cook bacon rashers on a plate or shallow dish, covering them loosely with absorbent kitchen paper to prevent spattering. Alternatively the rashers can be cooked on a special microwave roasting rack which allows the fat to drain away. The timing depends on personal taste and on the water content of the rashers, particularly when cooking just two rashers.

Defrosting Bacon Rashers To defrost a block of frozen rashers, unwrap them and place on a plate. Cook on full for 30 seconds, then gently ease the rashers apart with the blade of a knife. Place those that can be removed from the microwave on absorbent kitchen paper, then continue defrosting the block for 15–30 seconds to separate the remaining rashers in the same way. The rashers should still be icy, but they will be thoroughly defrosted after standing for a few minutes.

Cooking Bacon Rashers Cook on full for the following times:

2 rashers – 1½–2 minutes	
4 rashers – 2–3 minutes	
6 rashers – 3½–4½ minutes	
8 rashers – 5–6 minutes	

Bacon Sandwiches Spread thick slices of buttered fresh bread with mustard. Sandwich the cooked bacon rashers between the bread and butter and eat at once. Also good sandwiched between slices of hot buttered toast!

Bacon Rolls Halve rindless bacon rashers and roll up neatly. Secure with wooden cocktail sticks and place as far apart as possible on a plate. Cover with absorbent kitchen paper and cook on full for the following times:

2 rolls – about 1 minute	
4 rolls – 1½–2 minutes	
6 rolls – 2½–3 minutes	
8 rolls – about 3½ minutes	

Crispy Bacon Bits Dice rindless bacon and place in a basin, separating the bits. Cook on full, stirring halfway through to separate the bits, following the timings below as a guide. The bacon should be very well cooked and shrunk so that the bits will become very crisp and dry when cool. Watch the bacon carefully so that it does not overcook. Use a draining spoon to lift the bacon from the basin and drain it on absorbent kitchen paper. Leave to cool completely. Use in salads, and as a topping, with or without soured cream, for jacket potatoes or other cooked vegetables.

100g/4oz – 4–6 minutes	
175g/6oz – 7–9 minutes	
225g/8oz – 10–11 minutes	

BAKED BEANS

Canned baked beans can be heated in the micro-wave. Turn them into a basin and cover it with a plate as they tend to spatter and can make a mess inside the microwave. Cook on full as follows:

227g/8oz can – 2–2½ minutes	
425g/15oz can – 4–5 minutes	

Stir halfway through heating and again before serving.

BANANAS

Hot 'baked' bananas are delicious for pudding with custard, cream, yogurt – or even with ice cream! Select firm, medium or large bananas, peel them and sprinkle with lemon juice. Place in a shallow dish and trickle over a little golden syrup or honey, or dot them with jam. Cook on full, using these times as a guide:

1 – 1–1½ minutes	
2 – 2–3 minutes	
3 – 3½–4 minutes	
4 – 4½–5 minutes	

The exact time depends on the size and ripeness of the fruit. Serve immediately and remember, hot bananas are very hot!

BARBECUE SAUCE

Crush a large clove of garlic into a basin and stir in 1 tablespoon tomato ketchup, 2 tablespoons tomato purée, 2 tablespoons sunflower oil, 1 tablespoon grated onion, 2 tablespoons Dijon mustard (or other mild mustard), 2 tablespoons cider vinegar, 2 tablespoons demerara sugar, 150ml/¼ pint water and a dash of Worcestershire sauce. Heat on full for 2–3 minutes, stir well and taste for seasoning. Serve with grilled or barbecued poultry, burgers or meats. Alternatively, brush the sauce over the raw foods before they are barbecued, grilled or baked. This sauce is also good brushed over chicken portions before cooking in the microwave (see page 40).

BASMATI RICE
See Rice, page 132.

BATTENBURG CAKE
Basic cake mixtures are trimmed and wrapped in almond paste to make this famous cake. Because of the trimming and decoration this cake can look – and taste – as good as when cooked by traditional methods.

Cream 100g/4oz soft margarine with 100g/4oz caster sugar, then stir in 2 eggs and fold in 100g/4oz self-raising flour. Grease two 13 × 19cm/5 × 7½ in loaf dishes and line their bases with greaseproof paper, then grease the paper. If you have only one dish, then simply wash the dish before cooking the second batch of cake. Place half the mixture in one dish and cook on full for 2–3 minutes, or until the cake is risen and springy but still slightly moist on top. Leave in the dish for 3 minutes, then turn out and cool. Colour the second half of the mixture pink by adding a few drops of red food colouring. Cook in the same way.

Trim the cooled cakes and halve them lengthways, then sandwich the four long strips together with a little apricot jam, chequerboard style. Spread jam thinly around the outside of the cake and wrap completely in rolled out almond paste (you will need about 350g/12oz to go round the cake). Finally sprinkle with caster sugar.

BATTERS

See Combination Microwave Cooking, page 50.

Batters rely on heat to crisp the outside, to hold the rise and to give good results, therefore they do not cook successfully in the ordinary microwave. Unless you have a combination microwave oven, avoid toad-in-the-hole, Yorkshire pudding, batter puddings and pancakes.

BEANS, DRIED

Dried beans and pulses can be cooked in the microwave but they need lengthy cooking, as by conventional methods. If you do cook dried beans in the microwave, then use a large bowl – a suitable mixing bowl is ideal – and add plenty of boiling water from the kettle. Do not salt the beans before cooking and cover the bowl (a plain heatproof dinner plate is ideal if there is no lid). If the beans have been pre-soaked, then cook on medium-high for about two-thirds of the conventional cooking time, checking frequently to ensure that there is plenty of liquid and topping up with fresh boiling water as necessary. If the beans have not been pre-soaked, then cook on medium-high for the same length of time as needed for conventional methods.

> *It is essential that red kidney beans are brought to the boil on full before the power is reduced to medium-high for the main part of the cooking. Watch the beans closely and make sure that they boil rapidly for 5 minutes. This kills natural toxins that are present in the beans.*

Canned beans and pulses can be heated in the microwave or used in dishes such as chilli con carne. The beans are already cooked and they simply need brief reheating. A 425g/15oz can of pulses (red kidney beans, chick peas, borlotti beans, butter beans etc) should be heated with the liquid from the can, in a covered dish on full for 3–4 minutes.

BEANS, FRESH OR FROZEN

All types of fresh or frozen beans cook well in the microwave, retaining the maximum flavour and nutrients, as well as colour.

The only exception to this rule are older runner beans that have become slightly stringy – when boiled by traditional methods they tenderise but they do not cook well in the microwave. Tender young runner beans are delicious cooked in the microwave. Cook on full, in a covered dish, adding 3 table-spoons water to fresh beans. Do not add salt. Halfway through cooking stir or rearrange the beans – this is more important when cooking larger quantities. Cut French beans cook slightly more quickly and evenly than the whole ones. The timing for frozen vegetables is not in proportion to that for fresh ones as the frozen types usually take less cooking, because they have been parboiled before freezing.

Broad Beans

100g/4oz	shelled fresh	3–4 minutes
225g/8oz	shelled fresh	6–7 minutes
450g/1lb	shelled fresh	9–10 minutes
100g/4oz	frozen	4–5 minutes
225g/8oz	frozen	7–8 minutes
450g/1lb	frozen	11–12 minutes

French Beans

100g/4oz	fresh	3–4 minutes
225g/8oz	fresh	5–7 minutes
450g/1lb	fresh	7–10 minutes
100g/4oz	frozen	4–5 minutes
225g/8oz	frozen	7–9 minutes
450g/1lb	frozen	12–14 minutes

Runner Beans

100g/4oz	fresh	2–3 minutes
225g/8oz	fresh	4–5 minutes
450g/1lb	fresh	6–7 minutes
100g/4oz	frozen	3–6 minutes
225g/8oz	frozen	6–8 minutes
450g/1lb	frozen	8–10 minutes

Note *Home-frozen runner beans that are in a block should be broken up as they defrost. They take longer to defrost and cook than purchased frozen beans.*

BEAN SPROUTS

To retain their crunchy texture bean sprouts should be cooked very briefly. They are usually combined with a variety of other ingredients and should always be added towards the end of the cooking time, so that they are heated for about 1 minute on full, depending on the quantity and type of recipe.

Simple Chop Suey Halve, then thinly slice 1 onion and place in a bowl with 2 tablespoons oil. Cut 1 medium carrot into fine strips and add to the onion. Cover and cook on full for 4 minutes. Stir in 50g/2oz frozen peas and 1 tablespoon soy sauce and cook on full for 2 minutes. Toss in 225g/8oz fresh bean sprouts, cover and cook on full for 1 minute, then stir and serve.

BÉCHAMEL SAUCE

Place 40g/1½oz plain flour in a basin and gradually mix in 600ml/1 pint milk, first to make a smooth paste, then adding the milk more quickly and whisking all the time. Add a bay leaf, blade of mace, seasoning and a good knob of butter. Cook on full for 7–10 minutes, until the sauce has thoroughly boiled and thickened. Whisk the sauce thoroughly after about 2–3 minutes, when it is just beginning to thicken, and scrape any bits of flour from the basin as you whisk. Whisk well before serving, remove the bay leaf and mace and taste for seasoning. For a plain, savoury white sauce omit the bay leaf and mace.

Cheese Sauce Whisk in 100g/4oz grated matured Cheddar at the end of the cooking time. The cheese should melt without having to be heated further.

Mushroom Sauce Add 175g/6oz whole button mushrooms to the cooked sauce. Cook for a further 1 minute on full before serving.

Onion Sauce Finely chop 1 large onion and cook with a good knob of butter or margarine on full for 3 minutes. Stir in the flour, then work in the milk and continue as above.

Parsley Sauce Add plenty of chopped fresh parsley to the cooked sauce – about 4–6 tablespoons.

BEEF

Combined with onions, vegetables and other ingredients in a sauce, minced beef and tender frying steak can be cooked very successfully in the microwave. Joints of beef can be cooked by microwave only but the result cannot be compared favourably to a traditional roast; however, the acceptability of a microwave-cooked joint depends on individual taste. Boned and rolled joints cook better than beef on the bone. The cooking times given can be used as a guide if you want to cook a joint completely in the microwave; a medium setting is best for large joints, to allow time for the meat to cook through without overcooking on the outside. Small joints can be cooked on full.

> *As an alternative to cooking the joint completely in the microwave, why not part cook it in the microwave on full, then transfer it to a hot oven to finish off? This reduces the cooking time considerably without forfeiting quality.*

Tougher cuts of beef used in casseroles and stews do need long slow cooking for the best results but, again, these dishes can be cooked in the microwave and the acceptability of the results is a question for personal preference. It is not recommended to try stewing steak but braising steak can be cooked on a medium or medium-low microwave setting. The cooking time is shorter than by conventional methods and the meat will be just tender but still slightly chewy at the end of cooking. If you prefer very tender, full flavoured, rich beef stews and casseroles, then it is best to cook them by traditional methods. See Pressure Cooker, page 126.

Defrosting Beef The microwave is very useful for defrosting all cuts of meat, from mince to a joint. Unwrap the meat and place it in a dish. Cover and cook on defrost setting for the recommended length of time. Turn a joint frequently during defrosting and shield any small areas that look as if they are beginning to cook by placing a small piece of smooth foil over them. At the end of the defrosting time the joint should still be slightly icy and it should be left to stand for 10–15 minutes before cooking. If you are defrosting a block of beef steaks, then separate them as soon as possible during the defrosting time. A block of minced beef should be broken up as it defrosts and any loose mince that is beginning to get warm should be removed from the microwave and set aside. Cubes of beef defrost well, they should be separated as soon as possible if they are in a block and they should be turned and rearranged at least once during defrosting.

Defrosting times per 450g/1lb beef:

Joints	8–10 minutes
Steaks (depending on size and thickness)	4–8 minutes
Cubes	7–9 minutes
Mince	8–10 minutes

Cooking Beef
Cooking times per 450g/1lb beef on medium:

Joints,	rare	10–12 minutes
	medium	13–15 minutes
	well done	14–16 minutes
Braising steak		16–18 minutes (allow 20–21 minutes on medium-low)

Cooking times per 450g/1lb beef on full:

Joints,	rare	5–6 minutes
	medium	6–8 minutes
	well done	8–9 minutes
Mince		10–15 minutes (timing for mince depends on other ingredients added)
Steaks		2–4 minutes

(steaks cook so quickly
under a hot grill that it
is best to cook them
conventionally)

Combining the microwave and oven An example of
how to part cook a roast in the microwave before
finishing it in the conventional oven: take a
1.5kg/3lb boned and rolled joint of beef and cook in
the microwave for 20 minutes on full, turning once
during cooking. Preheat the conventional oven to
220 C, 425 F, gas 7, then transfer the part-cooked
joint to the oven and cook for a further 10–30
minutes, depending on how rare or well cooked you
like your beef.

Bolognese Sauce Mix a finely chopped onion, 1
diced carrot, 1 chopped green pepper and 1 crushed
clove garlic in a casserole with 1 tablespoon oil.
Cover and cook on full for 5 minutes. Add 450g/1lb
minced beef, stir, then cover and cook on full for 3
minutes. Stir in a 400g/14oz can chopped tomatoes,
300ml/½ pint red wine or beef stock, salt and
pepper, 1 teaspoon dried marjoram and a bay leaf.
Cover and cook for a further 10–12 minutes on full,
stirring once. Stir well and taste for seasoning before
serving with cooked pasta.

Hamburgers, frozen Frozen burgers can be cooked
without defrosting first; place them as far apart as
possible on a flat dish and cover loosely with
absorbent kitchen paper. The result should not be
compared with a charcoal-grilled burger but it is
quite good enough for a hasty snack or meal. These
times are for cooking from frozen on full:

50g/2oz burgers

1 –	1½–2 minutes
2 –	3–4 minutes
4 –	4–6 minutes

100g/4oz burgers

1 –	2½–3½ minutes
2 –	5–6 minutes
4 –	8–10 minutes

Homemade Hamburgers Plain homemade all-meat hamburgers are best cooked on a barbecue or under the grill but this recipe cooks well in the microwave. Mix together 50g/2oz fresh breadcrumbs, 450g/1lb minced beef, 2 tablespoons tomato purée, a good dash of Worcestershire sauce, 1 teaspoon made English mustard, 1 teaspoon dried mixed herbs, 1 small egg and plenty of seasoning. Shape into four burgers and place as far apart as possible on a flat dish. Cook on full for 4–6 minutes.

BEETROOT
Fresh beetroot microwaves very well. Scrub the beets and trim off the leaves and root ends without cutting the beet. Do not peel. Place in a large dish or roasting bag and add 3 tablespoons water. Cover the dish or loosely close the bag with a microwave-proof tie or elastic band. Cook on full, allowing 5–7 minutes for 225g/8oz, or 9–11 minutes for 450g/1lb. Leave to stand for 5 minutes, then rub the skins off under cold running water. If the beetroot are large they may need to be cooked for a few minutes longer – when they are cooked the skins rub off easily.

BISCUITS
Traditional biscuit recipes do not cook well in the microwave – because of limited space only a few can be cooked at once and the result is far inferior to that which is expected from conventional methods. However, small cookies can be successful and they are an ideal recipe for children to try cooking.

Peanut Biscuits Cream 50g/2oz soft margarine with 50g/2oz crunchy peanut butter, 2 teaspoons grated orange rind, a few drops of vanilla essence and 2 tablespoons soft brown sugar. Work in 100g/4oz self-raising flour and 1 tablespoon water. Shape the mixture into ten small balls and place them on a greased dish, as far apart as possible. Flatten the biscuits with a fork and cook on full for 1½–2 minutes, until they are slightly risen and cooked. Leave them on the dish for 5 minutes, then transfer them to a rack to cool.

Drying Softened Biscuits *If biscuits or crackers have been left on a plate and become soft, then heat them for a few seconds on full and leave to cool, when they will crisp up again.*

BLACKBERRIES
The microwave is excellent for defrosting or cooking blackberries.

To defrost 450g/1lb fruit, place in a dish and cover. Allow about 5–7 minutes on defrost, stirring or gently breaking up a block of fruit halfway through the time.

To cook 450g/1lb blackberries, place in a dish with 100g/4oz sugar and cover. Cook on full for 6–8 minutes, stirring halfway through. Serve with custard or cream, or purée the fruit to make a delicious sauce for ice cream.

BLACKCURRANTS
Blackcurrants can be cooked from fresh or frozen in the microwave. Top and tail the fruit, then place in a dish with 100–175g/4–6oz sugar (to taste: if you are unsure, then use the smaller quantity and add extra when the fruit is cooked) and 2 tablespoons water. Cover and cook on full for 5–7 minutes. Stir

halfway through cooking and at the end of the time. To cook from frozen, allow an extra 1–2 minutes – the fruit softens during freezing, so it may not require lengthy extra cooking time.

BLANCHING
You can use the microwave to blanch small batches of vegetables before freezing. Prepare the vegetables according to their type, then follow the microwave cooking instructions, allowing about a quarter to one-third of the time suggested. The vegetables are ready when they are just beginning to cook. Plunge them immediately into iced water, then drain and dry thoroughly before packing and freezing.

BREAD
It is not possible to cook a traditional-style loaf successfully in the microwave. There are recipes that will work to produce a pale, close textured loaf which is nowhere near the standard expected from conventional cooking. However, by making a yeasted batter it is possible to produce a soft loaf with an acceptable texture and flavour. Use a 280g/10oz packet wholemeal bread mix and beat to a smooth elastic batter with 300ml/½ pint hand-hot water. Grease an 18cm/7in round dish and a 600ml/1 pint jug. Pour two-thirds of the batter into the dish and the remainder into the jug. Leave to rise to the tops of the containers in a warm place, then sprinkle with poppy seeds or toasted sesame seeds. Cook separately, on full, allowing 6–7 minutes for the dish and about 4 minutes for the jug. Leave in the containers for 5 minutes, then turn out to cool on a rack.

Defrosting Bread Place bread rolls as far apart as possible on absorbent kitchen paper on the floor of the oven or turntable. Heat on full for the following times:

1 – 15–30 seconds	
2 – 30–45 seconds	
3 – 1 minute	
4 – 1–1½ minutes	

Separate frozen sliced bread and place the slices as far apart as possible, overlapping them if necessary, on absorbent kitchen paper as for rolls. Rearrange the slices halfway through if defrosting more than two, then heat on full using these times as a guide:

1 – 15–30 seconds	
2 – 45 seconds	
3 – 1 minute	
4 – 1½ minutes	

To defrost an uncut loaf, unwrap it and place on a piece of absorbent kitchen paper in the microwave. Allow 7–10 minutes on defrost setting, depending on the size and shape of the loaf. Leave to stand for 10–15 minutes before cutting. A large loaf may still be firm in the centre, in which case heat for a few minutes on defrost when you reach the frozen part.

See also Pitta Bread, page 119.

BREADCRUMBS

You can dry fresh breadcrumbs in the microwave to make fine white crumbs. Place the fresh bread-crumbs in a bowl and cook uncovered on full for 2 minutes, then stir well and continue to cook for bursts of 1–2 minutes, depending on the quantity, until the crumbs are very hot and beginning to dry. Leave to cool if they are crisp and dry, as they are then ready for storing or using; if they are still slightly soft, repeat the cooking process. The dry crumbs will crush finely quite easily if you rub them between the palms of your hands.

BREAD SAUCE

Stud a peeled onion with 4 cloves and place it in a jug or basin. Cover and cook on full for 2 minutes, then add a bay leaf and 600ml/1 pint milk. Cook on full for a further 5–6 minutes, then stir in 100g/4oz fresh white breadcrumbs and seasoning to taste. Cook for a final 2–3 minutes before removing the onion and bay leaf. Taste to season before serving.

BROCCOLI

Fresh or frozen broccoli cooks well in the microwave.

> *To prevent the broccoli heads overcooking before the stalks are tender, arrange the stalks towards the outside of a round cooking dish and the heads together in the middle.*

Sprinkle with 4 tablespoons water and cover the dish. Cook on full following these times:

100g/4oz – 2–4 minutes	
225g/8oz – 5–6 minutes	
450g/1lb – 7–9 minutes	

Frozen Broccoli

225g/8oz – 7–8 minutes	
450g/1lb – 12–14 minutes	

Leave for 2 minutes before draining and serving.

BROWNIES

You can use the microwave to make a wickedly sticky version of chocolate brownies! Grease and base line an oblong dish measuring 20 × 13cm/8 × 5in and grease the lining paper well. Melt 50g/2oz butter with 100g/4oz soft brown sugar on full for 2 minutes. Beat in 75g/3oz self-raising flour,

40g/1½oz cocoa powder, 50g/2oz finely chopped walnuts and a beaten egg. Spread in the dish and cook on full for 1½–2½ minutes, until firm but still slightly sticky on top. Cool in the dish, then cut into squares when cold.

BROWNING DISH

A microwave cooking dish with a special coating over the base which absorbs microwave energy. The dish is heated empty according to the manufacturer's instructions until it becomes very hot. The food is then placed in the dish and it browns on the hot base. Useful for chops, steaks, for cooking fish fingers or similar, or sausages. The disadvantages are that most of the dishes are very expensive and the browning is minimal. Once the food is in the dish the hot base rapidly loses heat and to thoroughly brown two sides of the food it is necessary to empty and reheat the dish again before adding the food, second side down. Best to get to know your microwave and decide which foods you are going to cook frequently before buying this accessory.

BROWN RICE
See Rice, page 132.

BRUSSELS SPROUTS
No more soggy sprouts! The microwave makes easy work of cooking Brussels sprouts to perfection. Trim and thoroughly wash the vegetables, cutting a cross in the hard base of each. Place in a dish with 4 tablespoons water, cover and cook on full, stirring halfway through. The cooked sprouts should retain a bit of crunch. Follow these times as a guide:

100g/4oz – 2–3 minutes	
225g/8oz – 4–6 minutes	

450g/1lb – 8–10 minutes

Frozen Sprouts

100g/4oz – 3–5 minutes
225g/8oz – 7–8 minutes
450g/1lb – 11–12 minutes

Drain and toss in butter before serving. Good with almonds browned in butter (see page 6).

BUCKWHEAT
A small nutty grain which can be served instead of rice or added half-and-half to cooked rice to make a tasty side dish. Rinse 225g/8oz grain under cold water and drain. Cook 1 finely chopped onion with a good knob of butter on full for 3 minutes. Add the buckwheat, a little seasoning and 300ml/½ pint boiling water. Cover and cook on full for 3–5 minutes. Leave to stand for 5 minutes, then add plenty of chopped fresh parsley and fork up the grain before serving.

BUTTER
Frozen butter can be defrosted rapidly in the microwave: unwrap it, place on a plate and cook on full for 30–45 seconds (for 250g/8oz packet). The block will look hard on the outside but the centre will be very soft, so leave it to stand for 2 minutes before using. If you have more time, then allow about 2 minutes on medium.

> *Butter taken from the refrigerator can be heated in the microwave for just a few seconds to soften it for spreading.*

Do not forget the microwave when you are melting butter for cake making or for topping cooked vegetables (hot melted butter will keep freshly cooked vegetables hotter than cold knobs that are dotted over the top). Place the butter in a basin, jug or mug and cook on full until melted – about 30–45 seconds for 50g/2oz.

CABBAGE

All types of cabbage can be cooked successfully in the microwave, the most even results being achieved by shredding the vegetable finely before cooking. Put the shredded cabbage in a large dish with 4 tablespoons water, cover and stir halfway through cooking. Cook on full; the exact timing depends on taste, the following guide gives tender, crunchy results:

100g/4oz – 3–5 minutes
225g/8oz – 6–8 minutes
450g/1lb – 9–11 minutes

Frozen cabbage needs little cooking once it has defrosted so the above timings can be used.

Red Cabbage with Apple Cook 1 finely chopped onion and a good knob of butter on full for 3 minutes. Add 450g/1lb finely shredded red cabbage, 2 tablespoons demerara sugar, 25g/1oz raisins and 2 tablespoons water. Cover and continue to cook on full for 4 minutes. Peel, core and thinly slice a large cooking apple and add it to the cabbage with 1 tablespoon cider vinegar. Stir well, cover and cook on full for 3–5 minutes, or until the cabbage and apple are tender. Season before serving.

Stuffed Cabbage Leaves Trim the hard core off large

leaves, place in a roasting bag or large dish with 150ml/¼ pint water. Cover or close bag loosely with a microwave-proof tie or elastic band, then cook on full, allowing 1–2 minutes for 4 leaves, 3–5 minutes for 8 leaves. Rearrange the leaves halfway through. Prepare a filling using minced beef or pork, cooked with onion (see page 22), allowing 10 minutes per 450g/1lb (enough for 8 leaves). Stir in a few fresh breadcrumbs, chopped fresh parsley and chopped mushrooms, adding a little milk to bind and seasoning to taste. Divide between the leaves, roll into neat packages and arrange in a dish. Coat with Tomato Sauce (see page 148) or Béchamel Sauce (see page 20) and heat on full for 3–5 minutes. Sprinkle with cheese and brown under the grill before serving.

CAKES

It is possible to cook a creamed cake mixture in the microwave, either in paper cases to make buns, in a small round dish or in a ring dish. However, it has to be said that the result is inferior to that expected of traditional baked cakes, the only exception being a chocolate cake mixture. Plain mixtures turn out very pale and they have the flavour of a steamed pudding rather than a baked cake. They can be disguised by adding icing and decoration; their acceptability is open to personal preference and is usually related to the speed and ease with which they can be cooked. If you do want to make plain cakes, then follow the timings given for the chocolate cake below.

Chocolate Cake Make a one-stage mixture by beating together 100g/4oz soft margarine, 100g/4oz caster sugar, 100g/4oz self-raising flour, 4 tablespoons cocoa powder, 2 eggs and 4 tablespoons milk. Beat well until the mixture is very creamy and soft. Thoroughly grease a 900ml/1½ pint ring dish. Place half the mixture in the dish and cook on full for 3–3½ minutes, or until the cake is firm but still slightly moist on top. Leave for 2 minutes, then turn out on to a rack to cool. Wash, dry and grease the dish and cook the remaining mixture in the same way. When cool sandwich together with chocolate nut spread and coat with chocolate icing (see page 46). Alternatively, sprinkle each cake with a little kirsch or sherry. Sandwich together with black cherry conserve and cover with whipped cream. Sprinkle with grated chocolate and decorate with canned black cherries if you like.

Chocolate Buns Make a half quantity of the above cake mixture and divide it between 12 double thick paper cake cases. Cook the cakes four at a time, placing them as far apart as possible on a large plate, allowing 1–1¼ minutes on full for each batch. The cakes should be slightly moist on top when cooked. Ice with melted chocolate and top with walnut halves.

CANNELLONI
See Pasta, page 113.

CARAMEL
The microwave is great for making caramel but care must be taken to avoid disaster. The first stage of cooking the caramel, until all the sugar has melted and the syrup has reduced, takes some time (be patient!) but as soon as the mixture begins to caramelise you have to watch it very closely to prevent it from overcooking. The container must stand the heat of the caramel – ovenproof glass is suitable (for example, Pyrex jugs or basins). Remember to use an oven glove to lift the container.

Place 175g/6oz sugar in a suitable basin with

6 tablespoons water. Cook on full for 2 minutes, then stir well to dissolve the sugar. Continue to cook on full for a further 9–10 minutes. After 5–6 minutes you should stand near to make sure that the caramel does not overcook. As soon as you notice the syrup beginning to turn lightly golden in parts be ready to remove it from the microwave. It is ready when light to medium golden as it will continue to darken after it is removed from the microwave. If you want to keep the caramel runny, rather than letting it set hard, very carefully add 4 tablespoons boiling water from the kettle. Gently pour the water into the basin from the side as it will spit and steam.

CARROTS

New carrots and large fresh main crop carrots cook well in the microwave, but old, slightly dried out carrots are better cooked in boiling water on the hob. Trim and scrub new carrots, scrub or peel old carrots. Cut large carrots into even-sized pieces, either slices or matchstick strips (julienne). Place in a dish with 4 tablespoons water, cover and cook on full. The timing depends on the size of the pieces of vegetable – small new carrots, fine strips and thin slices cook quickly, thick slices take longer and chunks or quartered vegetables need the longest time. Stir the vegetables halfway through cooking.

100g /4oz – 2–3 minutes
225g/8oz – 4–5 minutes
450g/1lb – 6–8 minutes

Frozen vegetables need very little cooking once defrosted so follow the above timings but do not add extra water.

CAULIFLOWER

Cauliflower cooks very well in the microwave, either

left whole or broken into florets. Select a good, firm vegetable (those that are limp and old are best cooked in a saucepan of boiling water on the hob – if at all!) and place it in a dish with 4 tablespoons water. Cover and cook on full, following the times suggested below, then leave for 3 minutes before draining and serving. The result makes excellent cauliflower cheese which is not at all watery. Toss florets in butter and freshly ground black pepper before serving.

small whole cauliflower	10–12 minutes
large whole cauliflower	13–16 minutes
100g/4oz florets	4–5 minutes
225g/8oz florets	6–8 minutes
450g/1lb florets	10–12 minutes

Frozen florets need very little cooking once they have defrosted, so follow the above timings but do not add any extra water.

Cauliflower Cheese First prepare a cheese sauce (see page 20). Cover the surface of the sauce with buttered greaseproof paper, buttered side down, to prevent a skin forming. Cook a whole cauliflower or florets, whichever you prefer. Drain the cooking liquid from the cauliflower and stir it into the sauce, then pour the sauce over the cauliflower. Mix 25g/1oz fresh breadcrumbs with 50g/2oz grated cheese and season with a little freshly grated nutmeg if you like. Sprinkle this mixture over the coated cauliflower and brown it under a hot grill. Alternatively, use browned breadcrumbs or chopped walnuts and heat in the microwave on full for 1–1½ minutes before serving.

CELERIAC

This large root vegetable has the same flavour as

celery. It cooks just like potatoes, and is delicious cut into chunks and tossed in butter and snipped chives, or mashed with butter and black pepper. Alternatively, neat short strips can be served topped with soured cream and chopped spring onion. Peel the vegetable thickly, then cut it into even-sized pieces (chunks, strips or quartered slices). Place in a large dish, add 4 tablespoons water and cover. Cook on full, rearranging halfway through cooking.

450g/1lb	– 6–8 minutes
675g/1½lb	– 10–12 minutes
1kg/2lb	– 14–16 minutes

Braised Celeriac Cook a finely chopped onion in a knob of butter on full for 3 minutes. Add the diced celeriac and use chicken stock instead of water, stirring to mix. Add a bay leaf, cover and cook as above. Remove the bay leaf and stir in 2 tablespoons single cream with seasoning before serving. Sprinkle with chopped parsley if you like.

CELERY

Celery can be cooked in the microwave but the result depends on the preparation. Trim the stalks, cutting off blemished areas and peeling away strings.

> *For best results thinly slice the celery – if the stalks are cut into longer lengths, I find that microwave cooking tends to accentuate any stringy bits that have not been cut off.*

Place the slices in a large dish and toss in 4 tablespoons water. Cover and cook on full, stirring halfway through cooking.

225g/8oz	– 4–5 minutes
450g/1lb	– 8–10 minutes

Drain and serve tossed in butter and freshly ground black pepper. Alternatively, cook a chopped onion in butter for 3 minutes on full before adding the celery. Use medium-sweet cider instead of water and cook as above. Blend 1 teaspoon cornflour with 1 tablespoon cold water and stir into the celery for the last 2 minutes cooking. Season before serving.

CHEESE

Cheese heats rapidly in the microwave and it can be overcooked very quickly. When melting cheese on its own – as a topping for a snack or similar – time it very carefully for seconds instead of minutes. If there is a large area of cheese to be melted, then it is best to use medium power.

Cheese Fondue Use a microwave-proof fondue pot or a suitable bowl or dish. Heat 150ml/¼ pint dry white wine or cider with a crushed clove of garlic on full for 3 minutes, until very hot. Mix 450g/1lb grated cheese (preferably Gruyère) with 3 table-spoons plain flour and seasoning to taste. Gradually stir half the cheese into the hot wine or cider and cook for a further 2 minutes on full. Stir well, add the remaining cheese and flour mixture and mix thoroughly. Cook for 2 minutes. Stir again, and continue to cook for 2–4 minutes, until all the cheese has melted and the fondue is thick and smooth. Keep hot over a candle warmer or fondue burner. Serve chunks of crusty bread, apple and celery to dip into the fondue.

Cheese Sauce See page 20.

Cheese Straws Good when you are in a hurry, these do not brown but they are crisp and very more-ish! Beat 50g/2oz butter until soft, then work in 50g/2oz grated matured Cheddar cheese, 1 tablespoon grated Parmesan cheese, 2 teaspoons wholegrain mustard (or any other made mustard), 1 tablespoon snipped chives and 75g/3oz self-raising flour. Use your fingers to press the mixture together, then divide it into ten small balls. Shape each into a thin stick, about 15cm/6in long, and roll them in toasted sesame seeds, poppy seeds or paprika. Cook in two batches, arranging five straws as far apart as possible on a large flat dish. Allow 3–4 minutes on full for each batch. Leave on the dish for a minute or two, then cool the straws on a rack.

> **Warming Chilled Cheese** *Cheese taken from the refrigerator can be brought to room temperature by heating for 15–30 seconds on medium. Unwrap the cheese first and stand it on a piece of absorbent kitchen paper.*

Welsh Rarebit Traditionally heated in a saucepan before being grilled on toast, this works well in the microwave. Heat 50ml/2fl oz milk or beer on full for 1–2 minutes, until very hot. Mix 225g/8oz grated cheese with 2 teaspoons mustard powder and salt and pepper. Beat the cheese into the hot milk or beer and cook on full for 2–3 minutes. Beat thoroughly – the rarebit should be smooth and creamy. Spread on freshly buttered toast and brown under the grill. The cooled cooked rarebit can be kept covered in the refrigerator for 2 days, ready to spread on toast and pop under the grill to brown.

CHERRIES
Cook stoned or whole, fresh or frozen cherries in the microwave. Heat 100g/4oz sugar with 150ml/¼ pint water for 3 minutes on full. Stir until the sugar dissolves, then add the cherries and cover the dish before cooking. Stir in port, kirsch, brandy or sherry before serving.

450g/1lb fresh	– 3–4 minutes

| 450g/1lb frozen – 4–5 minutes |
| 675g/1½lb fresh– 5–6 minutes |

CHESTNUTS

Cook fresh chestnuts in the microwave. Wash them well and make a split in the shell of each one. Place in a dish, still wet from washing, and cover. Cook on full, allowing 4–6 minutes for 225g/8oz. Stir to rearrange halfway through cooking. Peel when cool enough to handle.

Chestnut Stuffing Cook 225g/8oz chestnuts as above, then peel and chop them. Finely chop 1 large onion and 100g/4oz rindless bacon and cook with a large knob of butter on full for 5–6 minutes, or until the bacon is just cooked. Mix with the chestnuts, 1 teaspoon dried sage, a pinch of dried thyme, 175g/6oz fresh breadcrumbs, salt and pepper and 4 tablespoons milk. Good for turkey or chicken or as a stuffing for large open mushrooms (see page 108).

CHICKEN

Chicken is tender, it cooks quickly and is a good candidate for microwave cooking. Whole birds, portions or chunks can be defrosted and cooked successfully.

Defrosting Chicken Calculate the time according to the weight of the bird or the portions. Unwrap a whole chicken and place in a dish. During defrosting the bird should be turned at least twice. If any areas – wings or legs – are beginning to get hot, cover with small pieces of foil to prevent them from cooking. Heat on defrost setting (or the setting suggested in your manufacturer's handbook for defrosting foods in your microwave), then leave to stand for 15 minutes at the end of the time. Remove the giblets from the chicken cavity – they should still be firm. The inside of the chicken should be very cold but not frozen and all the meat should be soft but not warmed. Cut away any fat from the body cavity of the bird and scald it with boiling water from the kettle if you intend to fill it with stuffing.

Portions should be unwrapped and placed on a dish for defrosting. They should be turned halfway through the time and left to stand for 5–10 minutes at the end of the time.

> *Boneless chicken breasts defrost very quickly and they are ready for cooking when still icy. For speed, small boneless breasts can be defrosted on full in bursts of 30 seconds.*

Times on Defrost Setting

Whole chicken and quarters	450g/1lb	7–9 minutes
Boneless breasts and small portions	450g/1lb	6–8 minutes

Cooking Chicken

Seasoning Do not sprinkle salt over chicken before cooking as this tends to result in dried-out spots. Pepper can be added before cooking and the liquid for casseroles can be lightly seasoned.

Covering A whole chicken and portions are best covered during cooking. Either use a large dish with a lid, a special domed microwave cover or a roasting bag. Drumsticks can be covered loosely with absorbent kitchen paper and casseroles should always be covered.

> **Arranging and Rearranging Portions**
> *Arrange portions so that the thin parts and the bone ends are together towards the middle of the dish. Thicker and meatier areas should be towards the outside of the*

> *dish where they get the most exposure to microwaves and cook more quickly. Half-way through cooking check to see if the pieces are cooking evenly, turn them over and rearrange them if necessary.*

Browning The skin does not brown but this can easily be remedied by placing the cooked chicken under a hot grill for a minute or two before serving. Alternatively, the skin can be removed from the portions before they are cooked in a casserole-type recipe.

Cooking a Whole Chicken Truss the chicken neatly, tying wings and bones close into the body to make the shape of the bird as even as possible. Weigh the chicken and calculate the cooking time following the guide given below. If the bird is to be stuffed, it should be weighed after stuffing. Place in a dish, breast up, and brush with oil or dot with butter. Cover and cook on full for 5–7 minutes. Turn the bird over so that the breast is underneath, then continue to cook for the remaining time. Leave to stand for 5 minutes before serving.

> **Shielding** *If you are cooking a large bird, then some bits may start to overcook before the rest of the chicken is ready, for example the leg ends and wing tips. Small pieces of smooth foil, shiny side outwards, can be placed over these areas to prevent them from cooking further.*

Testing the Cooked Bird It is essential that chicken is cooked through; check when the chicken has been standing for 5 minutes after cooking. Pierce the thick meat behind the thigh of the chicken: when cooked there should be no sign of blood and the meat should be juicy but not red. Test portions by piercing the meat at the thickest part. If you do not want to spoil the appearance of the chicken, then portions can usually be pierced from underneath.

Cooking Times on Full Power

Whole chicken	per 450g/1lb	7–9 minutes
Quarters	1	5–7 minutes
	2	10–12 minutes
	3	15–18 minutes
	4	21–25 minutes
Thighs or drumsticks	1	2–3 minutes
	2	4–6 minutes
	3	5–7 minutes
	4	7–10 minutes
	6	14–16 minutes
	8	18–22 minutes
Boneless breasts	1	2–4 minutes
	2	5–8 minutes
	3	9–11 minutes
	4	12–15 minutes

Flavouring Ingredients Place a small peeled onion studded with cloves and a halved orange or lemon in the body cavity of a whole chicken. For full flavour cook these ingredients first on full for 1 minute. Use bay leaves, sprigs of tarragon, thyme, sage or rosemary with chicken, either whole or portions. Tuck herbs into whole chickens, under or around portions, or under the skin of breasts.

Chicken Casserole Use this method as a guide for casseroling chicken, varying the flavouring ingredients and liquid. For a coq au vin, use red wine instead of stock and marinate the chicken portions in the wine overnight, then drain them before cooking. Cider can also be substituted for the stock. If using wine or cider, heat it separately before adding to the casserole so as not to increase the cooking time significantly.

Cook 1 chopped onion, 1 sliced stick celery, 1 sliced red pepper, 100g/4oz chopped rindless bacon and 1 tablespoon oil in a dish on full for 5 minutes. Stir in 2 tablespoons flour and 150ml/¼ pint boiling stock taken from 600ml/1 pint. Add 4 skinned chicken quarters, placing the meaty side up and the thicker parts to the outside of the dish. Cover and cook on full for 5 minutes. Turn the chicken over, stir in the remaining stock and add a bay leaf, sprig of parsley and sprig of thyme. Add a little seasoning to the liquid and stir. Cover and cook on full for 14 minutes. Add 100g/4oz sliced closed cup mushrooms and cook for a further 2–3 minutes, until the chicken is cooked. Sprinkle with chopped parsley before serving.

CHICKEN LIVERS
These cook well in the microwave. They are surrounded by a thin membrane so they must be halved or cut up before cooking to prevent bursting. Always cover the dish as they tend to spatter. Cook with a little butter, flavour with finely chopped onion and herbs to serve on toast, dice and add to cooked rice for a quick risotto, or use to make pâté.

Defrosting Chicken Livers Remove the lid from a 225g/8oz tub and heat on defrost setting for 5–7 minutes.

Cooking Chicken Livers The following is a guide to times on full power:

225g/8oz – 2–4 minutes	
450g/1lb – 5–7 minutes	

Chicken Liver Pâté Cook 450g/1lb chicken livers with 1 crushed clove garlic and 100g/4oz unsalted butter. They will need about 7–8 minutes on full, stirring halfway through cooking. Purée the cooked livers, adding 2 tablespoons brandy or sherry and seasoning to taste. Divide between four individual dishes or set in one dish. Cool, then top with melted butter and chill.

CHICK PEAS
See Beans, dried, page 17.

Canned chick peas are delicious, nutritious and versatile – they can be combined with cooked mince, vegetables, pasta, diced ham or spices. The canned variety can be heated rapidly in the microwave but the dried type really need to be pre-soaked and cooked for a long time, following the guidelines for dried beans (see page 17). As with other dried beans and pulses, chick peas can be cooked just as easily by boiling on a conventional hob.

CHICORY
Select small neat heads of chicory for microwave cooking, trim the ends and place in a dish. Sprinkle with 1 tablespoon lemon juice and 2 tablespoons water. Cover and cook on full, allowing 2–3 minutes for 2 pieces and 4–6 minutes for 4 pieces. Leave for 2 minutes, then drain and serve. Good coated in a cheese sauce (see page 20), or sprinkled with fresh breadcrumbs and cheese, and grilled to brown.

CHINESE LEAVES
These can be eaten raw in salads or they should be lightly cooked. For cooking, shred the head of

leaves, then wash well. Place in a large bowl, still damp and cover. Cook on full, stirring halfway through cooking, and allowing 4–5 minutes for 450g/1lb. Drain and toss with butter and chopped spring onions or parsley.

CHIPS

Frozen oven chips can be heated in the microwave – the result is what I call 'emergency food', acceptable when there's no time to spare and everyone's hungry but not to be compared with crackly crisp, old-fashioned, deep fried chipped potatoes! Spread the frozen chips out on a dish and heat on full as follows:

100g/4oz – 1½–2½ minutes	
175g/6oz – 3–4 minutes	
225g/8oz – 5–6 minutes	

CHOCOLATE

The microwave makes melting chocolate easy – no more pans of water and wet-bottomed basins. If you are melting large quantities, then the majority of advice indicates that medium is the safest setting to use. I have always had success with melting chocolate on full by watching it very closely and checking every 30–45 seconds, but this does depend on the performance of the individual microwave cooker. Break the chocolate into squares and stir gently once or twice during heating. The squares of chocolate retain their shape as they melt – so do not be deceived by appearance and do check for progress. The following times are a guide on full power.

100g/4oz – about 1 minute	
175g/6oz – about 2 minutes	
225g/8oz – about 2½–3 minutes	

Chocolate Icing Break 175g/6oz plain chocolate into a basin. Add 50g/2oz butter, 2 tablespoons milk and 4 tablespoons sifted icing sugar. Heat on full for 2–2½ minutes, stirring halfway through. Stir lightly and heat for a further 30 seconds if necessary; use at once.

Chocolate Sauce Break 175g/6oz plain chocolate into a basin. Add 50g/2oz butter and 4 tablespoons golden syrup. Heat on full for 2–3 minutes, stirring halfway through. Stir well and serve. Leftover sauce can be stored in an airtight jar in the refrigerator for up to 2 weeks, ready to be heated in the microwave. The sauce reheats quickly; so time it in seconds.

CHOUX PASTRY

This does not cook in the microwave. It will puff up and rise but the lack of heat to crisp the pastry means that as soon as the power is switched off the pastry sinks back to a leathery lump! Used in a gougère (a savoury dish consisting of a ring of choux pastry filled with vegetables, fish or meat in a sauce) it can be cooked with moderate success in a combination microwave, but plain choux buns or éclairs will not work even in the combination oven.

CHUTNEY

See also Piccalilli, page 118; Sterilising Jars, page 143.

The microwave is not suitable for cooking large quantities of preserves; however a small amount of chutney can be cooked in a mixing bowl or large casserole. It is particularly useful if you want to prepare an unusual chutney, such as mango chutney, in small quantities, or if you just want to make one or two pots of apple chutney.

Apple Chutney Mix 1 finely chopped large onion with 450g/1lb peeled, cored and roughly chopped cooking apples in a bowl. Add 50g/2oz roughly chopped raisins, a good pinch of chilli powder, 1 teaspoon ground ginger, 1 small chopped clove garlic, ½ teaspoon ground cinnamon and a pinch of ground cloves. Stir in 100g/4oz brown sugar, a good pinch of salt and 250ml/8fl oz malt vinegar. Make sure that there is plenty of room for the chutney to boil and to stir it well. Cook on full for 10 minutes, stir well, then cook for a further 7–10 minutes, or until the chutney is thickened. Pot, label and store for 2 weeks before sampling.

Mango Chutney You need small, hard, green mangoes for this (from ethnic grocers). Peel, stone and slice 675g/1½lb green mangoes and place in a bowl with 1 large finely chopped onion, 1 deseeded and chopped green chilli, 1 teaspoon salt, 3–4 crushed cloves garlic and 1 tablespoon ground coriander. Stir in 175g/6oz demerara sugar and 150ml/¼ pint malt vinegar. Cover and cook on full for 8 minutes. Uncover and cook for a further 7–9 minutes on full, stirring frequently, until the mangoes are tender. Pot and label, then mature for 2 weeks.

CHRISTMAS CAKE

It is not possible to achieve a good result when cooking a traditional Christmas cake recipe in the microwave – the ingredients are not cheap and it is better to cook the cake conventionally.

CHRISTMAS PUDDING

Small Christmas puddings can be cooked in the microwave with reasonable success. It is not worth trying to cook large puddings as the result is poor. This small pudding is perfect for two – make it at least a month before Christmas, adding a few drops of brandy or rum now and then to keep it happy as it matures!

Roughly chop 50g/2oz each of raisins, sultanas, currants, dates and dried apricots. Mix with the grated rind and juice of 1 small orange, ½ teaspoon ground mixed spice, 2 tablespoons brandy or rum, 25g/1oz ground almonds, 25g/1oz muscovado sugar, 1 beaten egg, 2 tablespoons shredded suet and about 50g/2oz fresh breadcrumbs. Pound all the ingredients together with a wooden spoon to make a moist mixture. If it is a little wet, then cover and leave to stand for 15–30 minutes or add just a few extra breadcrumbs. Press into a greased 600ml/1 pint basin, smoothing the top. Cover with a plate and cook on full for 3–5 minutes, or until the pudding is firm and cooked through. Cover the top of the pudding with a circle of waxed paper, waxed side down, pressing it on to the surface of the pudding. Wrap tightly in foil to exclude all air when cold. Store in a cool place to mature.

To reheat, remove the foil and paper. Cover with a plate and cook on full for about 2 minutes.

Note The possible dangers of cooking Christmas puddings in the microwave have been greatly publicised and they should not be ignored. Stay near the oven for the few minutes needed to cook the pudding; check halfway through the time to make sure that it is not overcooking and all will be well.

CLEANING THE MICROWAVE

As with all kitchen equipment, it is important for the purpose of good hygiene to keep the inside and outside of the microwave very clean. It is also important to ensure that the door area is kept free of any build up of dirt and spillage. It is essential to read and follow the manufacturer's instructions about care of the appliance. As a general guide, most turntables can be removed, washed and dried and replaced in the oven. Clean up any spillages immediately. Wipe the sides, all round the base and the roof of the oven with a damp cloth and the type of cleaning agent suggested by the manufacturer – this is usually a non-scratch liquid or similar. Wipe again with a clean damp cloth.

If you find that there is a lingering odour in the microwave – perhaps of onions, garlic or vinegar – then place a quartered lemon in a basin with plenty of cold water and heat until the water boils. Leave for 15 minutes, then heat again for 5 minutes and leave the door closed with the lemon water in the oven for at least 30 minutes. Heat once more until the water boils, then remove the basin and wipe the oven cavity with a clean, hot damp cloth. Leave the door open for a while and the smell should have gone. If the odour still lingers, then leave a cut lemon on a plate overnight in the oven (switched off, of course) with the door closed.

CLING FILM
Do not use ordinary cling film in the microwave as there is a danger of plastic molecules being deposited on the food, causing a risk to health. Special film is produced for use in the microwave and this is useful for covering dishes which do not have lids.

COCONUT
Desiccated coconut, or long thread coconut, can be browned in the microwave. Spread the coconut out on a dish and cook on full, allowing about 5 minutes for 100g/4oz, and stirring every minute. Watch the coconut as it cooks. Leave to cool before storing in an airtight jar, and use to decorate cakes.

COD
See Fish, page 74.

Fresh or frozen, cod fillets, steaks or chunks all cook well in the microwave. Follow all the instructions and timings given for fish.

COFFEE
Heat fresh coffee or make a mug of instant coffee in the microwave. To make a mug of instant, place the coffee in a suitable mug (remember, no metal decorations) and stir in cold water. Heat on full for 45–65 seconds, or until the coffee is very hot. Stir well to dissolve the coffee.

The microwave is useful for reheating coffee – have fresh coffee prepared at the beginning of a dinner party, ready to pop in the microwave before serving. Remember to avoid any pots which are trimmed with metal. It is also best to avoid pots which have long, thin spouts as there can be a build up of heat in the body of the pot, causing the coffee to spurt noisily out through the spout and all over the oven cavity! Allow about 7–9 minutes on full to heat 1.15 litres/2 pints cold, ready-made coffee. Heating by the mug takes about 45–60 seconds per mug.

COLEY
See Fish, page 74.

Coley fillet, pre-formed frozen steaks or chunks of this fish can be cooked in the microwave, following all the instructions and timings for fish.

COMBINATION MICROWAVE COOKING
A combination microwave cooker combines microwaves with conventional heat in the same oven cavity, to be used simultaneously. The majority of these appliances are roughly the same size as the

average microwave cooker but there are also full-sized conventional ovens which incorporate the facility for microwave cooking.

Advantages All the characteristics expected of traditional oven cooking can be achieved and the cooking time is speeded up by using microwave energy. Food browns and becomes crisp, and the resulting flavour can be compared favourably to traditional methods. Many foods which are not acceptable when cooked by microwaves alone are excellent when cooked by this method. Read and follow your manufacturer's instructions and suggested cooking times. Some foods which cook especially well by the combination method are listed below with guidelines for success.

Cooking Modes Combination ovens can be used for different cooking operations: as a basic microwave, using this energy source only and following all the rules that apply; as a fan oven using conventional heat only (most are convection ovens, with the hot air being re-circulated by a powerful fan, thus speeding up cooking); as a combination oven with the microwaves and conventional heat working at the same time. Some models have grills which can be used on their own or at the same time as the microwave energy. Many additional features are available, including pre-programmed settings for roasting meat or poultry or for cooking a variety of dishes.

Use of Metal Unlike the majority of basic microwave ovens, combination ovens often come with metal racks. Always follow the manufacturer's instructions for using the accessories which come with the oven – if you are unsure about any of the instructions, then do write to the manufacturer and ask for help. Many instruction books point out that metal baking tins which are filled with food can be used when cooking on the combination mode. There may not be a danger to the oven but I have found that because the microwaves do not pass through the sides and base of the container the results are not well cooked. To maximise the use of the microwave energy as well as the conventional heat it is best to use ovenproof glass and baking dishes.

Cooking Instructions and Results When cooking on combination mode the majority of foods and dishes are cooked using medium microwave setting and conventional heat. The temperatures selected for the conventional heat are usually quite high by comparison to traditional methods – the microwave energy speeds up the cooking process, so a hotter oven is needed to brown and crisp the food in the shorter time. The necessity for preheating these ovens seems to vary according to the model, and also the food being cooked; follow the manufacturer's instructions until you are experienced enough to judge for yourself.

The following foods are those that are usually not as good cooked by microwaves alone but excellent cooked on combination mode.

Meat Roasts very well. Use medium (or some manufacturers recommend a low setting) and a hot oven. There is no need to cover the joints but they must be turned to ensure even cooking. A short standing time is necessary before serving and it is best to season after cooking. There is no need to preheat the oven for roasting joints taking over 30 minutes. The following times are a guide to the minutes per 450g/1lb:

Beef

Joints:
topside
sirloin

rolled rib (off the bone)	180 C/medium	12–15 mins

Steak:		
medium to well done (not recommended for rare)	240 C/medium (preheat oven)	5–8 mins

Lamb

Leg	190 C/medium	9–11 mins
Shoulder	200 C/medium	10–12 mins
Breast (boned and rolled)	220 C/medium	12–14 mins

Pork

Loin (boned and rolled	220–190 C/medium (reduce temp after 10 mins)	14–16 mins
Loin – on the bone	220–190 C/medium (reduce temp after 5 mins)	14–16 mins
Leg	220-180 C/medium (reduce temp after 5 mins)	15–16 mins
Chops	240 C/medium (preheat oven)	7–9 mins

Pastry Shortcrust, puff and flaky pastries all cook very well to give crisp, light results with good texture. Cook pastry flans, pasties and pies with success. Choux pastry does not cook well by this method. The following times are intended as a guide; exact timings depend on the particular ingredients used.

Shortcrust Pastry Flan 23cm/9in, to part-bake before filling, pricked all over, lined with greaseproof and dried beans	250 C/medium (do not preheat oven)	5 mins

Part-baked pastry, quiche Lorraine type filling (3 eggs plus 300ml/½ pint milk, cooked onion, cheese and ham or part-cooked bacon)	200 C/medium (preheat oven)	12–15 mins
Shortcrust Pastry Pie Top (pastry made with 175g/6oz plain flour, 75g/3oz fat)		
With cooked steak and kidney filling	220 C/medium (preheat oven)	15 mins
With half-cooked mince, onion and mushroom filling	200 C/medium (preheat oven)	20 mins
Cornish Pasties Raw filling × 4	220 C/medium (preheat oven, use rack for two-level cooking; swop dishes over half-way through time)	18–20 mins
Puff Pastry Pie Top With cooked filling	220 C/medium (preheat oven)	10 mins

Bread This cooks well, giving a good flavour, browned and crusty on top. The sides and underneath of the loaf tend to be soft and pale when cooked but this is not a significant disadvantage.

Dough made with 450g/1lb strong plain flour risen in 23cm/9in deep round dish	250 C/medium	10–12 mins
Half quantity of above, in 450g/1lb loaf dish	250 C/medium (preheat oven for both above)	7–9 mins

Cakes Creamed mixtures cook well on combination

mode to give brown tops and a good flavour. The sides and base are usually pale. Use baking dishes instead of tins, lining them first with greased greaseproof paper. Leave in the dish for a few minutes before turning out. Use a standard sandwich cake mixture, adding 2–4 tablespoons milk or extra liquid. Take care not to overcook as this results in a dry texture.

For example, to cook a mixture of 175g/6oz each fat, sugar and self-raising flour, 3 eggs and 2 tablespoons milk, baked in an 18cm/7in deep dish, allow 13–15 minutes on 220 C/medium. Preheat the oven first.

Batters Yorkshire pudding or sweet batter puddings cook well. Make a batter from 100g/4oz plain flour, 2 eggs, 300ml/½ pint milk and 2 tablespoons water. Heat a little fat in a flan dish, pour in the batter and cook at 250˙C/medium for 10–15 minutes. Preheat the oven first. For toad-in-the-hole, cook 450g/1lb sausages at 250 C/medium for 5 minutes. Add batter and continue to cook for 12–15 minutes – the result is excellent!

CONVENIENCE FOODS
The microwave is useful for heating canned foods, for making up packet soups and sauces, for heating ready-cooked chilled dishes (flans or cottage pies; pastry items become soft but are acceptable as emergency fare) and, of course, for cooking frozen foods.

> *When purchasing convenience foods do read the packets – you may be surprised at the number that give specific instructions for preparing in the microwave. Follow instructions on the packet as they have been tested for the particular product.*

The following dos and don'ts outline the approach to heating convenience foods:

* Remove wrapping and place food in suitable container.
* Remove metal or foil containers and clips – follow the microwave manufacturer's instructions with regard to this point.
* Cover food which should stay moist.
* Cover pastry items, breads or cakes with absorbent kitchen paper to absorb moisture.
* Check food frequently, rearranging or stirring as necessary for even heating.
* Always make sure that food is thoroughly heated before serving – cold areas should be stirred or rearranged and heating continued until all food has been heated through.
* Always stir soups well before serving to distribute any hot spots.

---

* *For convenience foods which you use often make a note of quantities and timings on a pad kept near the microwave.*

CORN-ON-THE-COB
See also Sweet Corn, page 145.

Whole cobs of corn cook well in the microwave. Remove the outer leaves and husks, trim the ends and wash well. Place in a dish or roasting bag and add 4 tablespoons water. Cover or secure with a microwave-proof tie or elastic band and cook on full, rearranging halfway through cooking.

Fresh cobs

1 cob	– 3–5 minutes
2 cobs	– 6–8 minutes
3 cobs	– 8–10 minutes

4 cobs – 11–13 minutes

Frozen cobs – do not add water

1 cob – 5–7 minutes
2 cobs – 8–10 minutes
3 cobs – 12–14 minutes
4 cobs – 15–17 minutes

Drain and serve with butter.

COURGETTES

These are delicious cooked in the microwave – crisp and full of flavour. Trim and slice them, then place in a dish with a knob of butter. Cook on full power, stirring halfway through.

225g/8oz – 2–4 minutes
450g/1lb – 4–6 minutes

Frozen courgettes tend to be watery, so do not add butter before cooking. They are very soft when defrosted and require very little cooking, so follow the longer times above. Drain and dot with butter when hot.

Stuffed Courgettes Halve 4 courgettes, scoop out their middles and chop the scooped out flesh. Mix it with 1 small finely chopped onion, 1 crushed clove garlic and a knob of butter. Cook on full for 5 minutes. Stir in 100g/4oz fresh breadcrumbs, 2 tablespoons grated Parmesan cheese and 3 tablespoons chopped fresh parsley or basil. Spoon this filling into the courgette shells, dot with butter and cook four at a time on full, allowing 3–5 minutes for each batch. The shells should be tender but not soggy, the filling hot.

COVERING

Foods that need to stay moist during cooking should be covered. Covering reduces the cooking time of some foods slightly by keeping the hot steam in the dish and this also promotes even cooking. For example foods cooked in sauces, fish, chicken portions and vegetables, are usually covered during cooking. Throughout this book, covering has been mentioned where it is necessary; where there is no comment the food can be left uncovered.

> *Casseroles with lids are ideal but if you do not have a lid for a dish, then try using a plain heatproof dinner plate – this can be inverted over shallow containers like flan dishes.*

Special microwave-proof cling film can be used to cover dishes, and roasting bags or boil-in-the-bags can be used instead of covered dishes for many foods.

CRAB
Add canned crab meat to Béchamel Sauce (see page 20) or Mushroom Sauce (see page 20), heat on full for 30–60 seconds and serve with pasta or rice.
Defrosting Crab Unwrap and place in a dish. Cover and use defrost setting. Allow 3–5 minutes for 225g/8oz. Turn halfway through defrosting. The defrosted crab should still be very cold; drain and pat dry on absorbent kitchen paper before use.

CRANBERRIES
Fresh or frozen cranberries can be cooked in the microwave but should always be placed in a covered dish as they tend to pop and spatter all over the oven cavity. To defrost frozen cranberries, place in a dish, cover and use defrost power. Allow 3–5 minutes for 225g/8oz. If the frozen berries are to be used in a sauce, there is no need to defrost them first; simply add a minute or so on to the cooking time and check carefully to ensure that they are cooked.

Cranberry Sauce Mix 100g/4oz cranberries and 100g/4oz sugar in a basin. Add 2 tablespoons orange juice and cover, then cook on full for 2½ – 3½ minutes, or until the cranberries are soft. Stir in 2 tablespoons port and leave to cool, covered, before serving.

CREAM

Frozen cream is a useful freezer standby. Defrost it rapidly in the microwave. Place the required number of sticks in a dish and use defrost setting, stirring halfway through. Towards the end of the time, check and stir, pressing any small lumps of frozen cream to blend them in. Leave for 5 minutes before using. Take care not to overheat the cream or it will separate.

600ml/1 pint (whole bag of sticks)	7–9 mins
300ml/½ pint (half bag)	3–5 mins
150ml/¼ pint (quarter bag)	2–3 mins

CROÛTONS

Croûtons are crunchy pieces of bread, usually very small dice, which are used as a garnish on savoury dishes or added to salads for texture. Traditionally they are fried but the small cubes of bread can be dried until crisp in the microwave. In this dry state they can be stored for several weeks in an airtight jar. Before use simply toss the croûtons in hot melted butter. For variety, add crushed garlic or chopped fresh herbs to the butter before tossing the croûtons.

Cut 3 medium-thick slices of bread into small dice and sprinkle these over absorbent kitchen paper on a flat dish. Cook on full for 2–3 minutes, or until dry. Remove from paper immediately and leave to cool. Store when cold and use dry or toss in melted butter before using.

Alternatively, cook the bread as above for 1 minute, cool, then toss in melted butter and cook for a further 2 minutes, or until the croûtons are very crisp and lightly browned. Use as required.

CRUMBLE TOPPINGS

Fruit crumbles rely on traditional baking for their dry texture and crisp, brown top; however, acceptable crumbles can be cooked in the microwave if you add ingredients that will improve the texture. If plain toppings consisting of half fat to flour, sweetened with sugar, are cooked in the microwave they tend to be moist and pale with a 'floury' flavour. Improve this by spreading a small amount of crumble in a fairly thin layer and use demerara sugar instead of white sugar. Mix in some chopped toasted hazelnuts or walnuts, a handful of crunchy breakfast cereal and a little chopped mixed peel – vary these ingredients, always considering that you are trying to give the topping a bit of crunch and a little zest to counteract the floury taste. Grated orange rind goes very well! For a 50g/2oz flour and 25g/1oz butter mixture, add about 50g/2oz nuts and 25g/1oz chopped mixed peel. Cook the fruit base before adding the topping, then allow about 3–4 minutes on full for the topping. Brown the top under a hot grill for even better results.

CUCUMBER

Although we usually tend to reserve this vegetable for salads, it makes an interesting hot vegetable and cooks well in the microwave. Finely chop an onion and cook with a knob of butter on full for 3 minutes. Peel a cucumber and cut it into 5cm/2in lengths, then quarter each piece. Pat dry on absorbent kitchen paper, add to the onion and pop a bay leaf in the dish. Cover and cook on full for 3–6 minutes. The cucumber should be hot and firm. Season with a little salt, grated nutmeg and freshly ground black pepper . Sprinkle with chopped fresh herbs before serving – dill, tarragon, basil or parsley all go well with cucumber, depending on the main dish. If you like, the cucumber can be topped with soured cream and warmed for a further 30 seconds.

CUMBERLAND SAUCE
A traditional accompaniment for ham, also good with pork or sausages. Mix 1 teaspoon cornflour to a paste with the grated rind and juice of 1 orange. Stir in 4 tablespoons redcurrant jelly, 2 tablespoons port and 150ml/¼ pint red wine. Heat on full for 4–6 minutes, whisking twice, until boiling and thickened.

CURRY SAUCE
Easy to make in the microwave, and with an authentic flavour, add cooked fish, prawns, chicken or vegetables to this sauce and heat briefly before serving with rice.

Finely chop 1 large onion and place in a dish with 2 crushed cloves garlic. Add 50g/2oz ghee or butter, or 3 tablespoons oil, 2 whole cardamoms, a cinnamon stick and 1 bay leaf. Cover and cook on full for 4 minutes. Stir in 2 tablespoons ground cumin, 4 tablespoons ground coriander and 1 teaspoon ground ginger. If you want a hot sauce add ½–1 teaspoon chilli powder at this stage. Pour in 300ml/½ pint boiling water from the kettle, stirring all the time. Cook on full for 3 minutes, then stir in a 400g/14oz can chopped tomatoes. Cook for a further 3 minutes on full, stir well, taste and adjust the seasoning before using as a base for a fish, meat or vegetable curry.

CUSTARD

Various types of custard cook well in the microwave – custard powder or eggs can be used to make a pouring sauce, or set custards can be cooked in the microwave.

Custard Powder Sauce Mix 2–4 tablespoons custard powder with 2–4 tablespoons sugar (or to taste) in a basin. Gradually stir in a little cold milk from 600ml/1 pint to make a smooth paste. Whisk in the remaining milk and cook on full for 5–7 minutes, whisking thoroughly twice during cooking. The custard should be boiling and thickened. Serve at once.

Egg Custard Sauce Mix 2 tablespoons cornflour with ½ teaspoon vanilla essence and 3 tablespoons sugar. Add a little cold milk from 600ml/1 pint and mix to a smooth paste, then whisk in the rest of the milk. Cook on full for 5–7 minutes, until boiling and slightly thickened. Lightly whisk 4 egg yolks in a small basin. Add a spoonful of the hot sauce and whisk lightly, then pour the egg mixture into the sauce and whisk thoroughly. The hot sauce should cook the yolks which will thicken and enrich it. If it is still slightly runny, then cook for a further 30 seconds by which time the custard should coat the back of a spoon. Serve at once. To make a thicker custard, for setting on a trifle for example, increase the quantity of cornflour to 4 tablespoons.

Egg Custard Whisk 2 small eggs with 2 tablespoons caster sugar and a few drops of vanilla essence. Heat 350ml/12fl oz milk on full for 2–4 minutes, until hot but not boiling. Pour the milk on to the eggs, whisking all the time. Divide between four ramekin dishes. Stand the dishes in a large round flan dish and pour boiling water into the outer dish. Sprinkle the tops of the custards with a little grated nutmeg and cook on full for 3–5 minutes, or until the custards are just set. Serve warm or leave to cool, then chill before serving.

Crème Caramel Prepare a caramel following the instructions on page 33. Pour the hot caramel carefully into four ramekin dishes, swirling it round to coat them completely; pour any extra into a jug and save to serve separately. Make the set custards as above and pour into the ramekins. Do not sprinkle with nutmeg. Cook as above. Cool, then chill overnight or for 24 hours. Invert the caramel custards on to individual serving plates and serve with cream.

D

DAMSONS
See Plums, page 120.

Damsons can be cooked in the microwave in the same way as plums but remember that they need extra sweetening. To make a delicious fool, purée the cooled cooked damsons and fold into chilled custard or whipped double cream.

DEEP FRYING
Never try to deep fry or cook food in large quantities of oil in the microwave. It is dangerous because the temperature of the oil cannot be controlled in the same way as it can on the conventional hob.

DEFROSTING
Microwave cookers have gained much fame for their ability to defrost food in a fraction of the time that it takes at room temperature. As well as defrosting

raw foods, remember that the microwave is particularly useful for defrosting and reheating ready cooked dishes.

First, read the manufacturer's instruction book — it will tell you which setting is designed for defrosting food on your model. This is usually a defrost setting or a low setting. Most microwaves come with a guide to defrosting times for a selection of basic foods as well as cooking times for some foods. Note this and use them as a guide. Throughout this book, defrosting times are given as appropriate with the food entries — these are a guide and you should take care to check the food frequently while it is defrosting, particularly when your microwave is new and you are first discovering just how it performs.

Preparing Food for Defrosting The majority of food should be unwrapped and placed in a suitable container. If the food is frozen to the carton, then heat on full for 30 seconds or until it can be released (remember not to put metal or foil wrappings in the microwave). When the food is to be defrosted and heated in one operation, for example vegetables, the container should be covered.

Arranging and Rearranging As when cooking, the food must be arranged to best advantage before defrosting in the microwave. Arrange thick parts that require most energy towards the outside of the dish. Thin parts and areas that require less energy should be placed together towards the centre of the dish, or they may be overlapped to prevent them from beginning to cook. Most food needs to be rearranged at least once during defrosting, usually more than that. Either turn and reposition portions or stir to rearrange smaller items.

Power Setting For best results food should be defrosted on the setting suggested by the manufacturer of the appliance; however we all know that there are days when 10 minutes before dinner there's not a scrap of food outside the freezer. Under such rushed circumstances it is possible to defrost and reheat a variety of foods on a medium, medium-high or even full setting. The rules are to use short bursts of energy; to stay near so that you can turn, break up and stir foods frequently; and to make sure that the dish you have elected to defrost by a hasty 'not-quite-by-the-book' method will stand up to the treatment. Casseroles and other sauced dishes, soups and thin (or shallow) items (shallow pasta bakes, flans and gratins) can usually be defrosted in haste without any great loss of quality. Really, whether you do this successfully depends on common sense – you must watch the food closely and you must break it up evenly. Obviously the preferable method is the slower one; these are emergency measures!

Standing Time When defrosting large items of food it is important to allow a resting period when any warmth that is generated within the food has time to dissipate to all corners of the portion or block. This is usually necessary at the end of the defrosting time; however, if the food looks as though areas are becoming warm, then do leave it to rest for a short time before continuing to defrost in the microwave.

Shielding When defrosting items like a chicken or joint of meat it is sometimes necessary to shield small areas that are likely to cook before the rest has defrosted. Cover them with small pieces of smooth foil which will reflect the microwaves off the area.

Separating Foods During defrosting, as the food begins to soften, individual items should be separated from a main block. Blocks of casseroles, soups, sauces etc. should be broken up.

Packing for Freezing and Microwave Cooking When you freeze food it is as well to consider the process of defrosting and reheating. For example, by open freezing foods like vegetables and fruit, small amounts can be removed from the pack as needed and defrosted with greater success in the microwave than a solid block of food. Simply freeze the food spread out on a tray, then pack it into bags when hard.

Casseroles can be packed in boilable bags or roasting bags, ready to go straight into the microwave for defrosting and reheating. Remove any metal ties and substitute with a microwave-proof tie or elastic band.

It is a good idea to label foods which you frequently freeze and reheat in the microwave with a note on the reheating time as well as the name of the dish and the date on which it was frozen. For example, if you make a certain recipe that freezes well, then take note of the best method of defrosting and reheating it in the microwave. When you next make and freeze the same recipe, add a label which gives instant information about how long to defrost on a certain setting and how long to reheat on full before serving. This is particularly useful with items like homemade cottage pie or lasagne which can take longer than expected to defrost and reheat.

Lastly, when freezing prepared dishes like lasagne, gratins and cottage pie, make sure that the dish will fit into the microwave for defrosting. This may seem obvious but I have packed soups into very tall containers and by the time the block of soup is turned into a bowl to defrost it is too tall for the microwave – infuriating!

> *If you do not want to leave favourite cooking dishes stacked away in the freezer, line them with microwave-proof film before putting in the food to freeze. When solid, use the film to ease the food out of its dish, wrap and label the block. To reheat, unwrap the food and replace in the dish. If the film is slightly stuck to the food, then pop the block in the microwave for 30–60 seconds on full and it should come off easily. If the food is cooked in the dish initially, it has to be removed, the dish washed and lined before the food can be replaced and frozen.*

DOUGH

Traditional yeasted doughs cannot be cooked in the microwave to anything like the same standard as expected conventionally, therefore this cooking method is not recommended. However, the microwave can be useful when preparing the dough. Warm the flour before adding any other ingredients by placing it in a bowl in the microwave and heating on full for 30–60 seconds. Stir it and feel with your fingers to see if it is pleasantly warm – the warmth will speed up the action of the yeast. The proving time for the dough can be shortened by placing it in the microwave and heating on medium for 30–45 seconds. Do this once or twice during proving to speed up the yeast – do not be tempted to lengthen the time or to use full power as this may kill the yeast or cook the dough.

DRINKS

See Coffee, page 50; Tea, page 146; Punch, page 128 and Honey Toddy, page 89.

Use the microwave to heat up a mug of coffee that

has been allowed to cool instead of pouring it down the sink. Heat individual glasses of mulled wine, warming whisky toddies or other individual drinks in the same way. Remember the rules: no metal, no cut glass, no fine bone china.

DUCK

Surprisingly, duck cooks very well in the microwave to give tender, juicy meat. A whole duck, or portions with skin on, need to be browned before serving. The result of combining microwave cooking with a very speedy period of browning in the hottest conventional oven is a duck which is succulent, full-flavoured and beautifully crisp – absolutely delicious!

Defrosting Duck Unwrap, place on a dish and allow 5–6 minutes per 450g/1lb on defrost setting. Turn the bird twice during defrosting and shield wing and leg areas with small pieces of foil if they become warm. Leave to stand for 15 minutes. Remove the giblets and cut away lumps of fat from the bird before scalding the body cavity with boiling water.

Cooking Whole Duck Weigh the bird and calculate the cooking time at 6–8 minutes on full per 450g/1lb. Prick the skin all over. Place a halved onion studded with 4 cloves and 2 bay leaves in the body cavity. Reserve the giblets for making stock. Place the duck in a dish, breast down, and cook on full for 5 minutes. Turn the bird over and cook for the remaining time. Drain excess fat from the cooking dish at least twice during cooking. The duck meat should be just cooked when removed from the microwave because it will continue cooking as the skin is browned. If you are using the oven method for browning then the meat can be very slightly pink at this stage. Test by piercing the thick part of meat behind the thigh of the duck. Drain the cooked duck thoroughly, blotting the skin with absorbent kitchen paper. Rub with salt and pepper to taste and brown under a moderately hot conventional grill, until crisp and golden, turning the duck once to brown the other side. Alternatively (and really the best, if not the most economical, method) put the duck in a conventional oven preheated to 240 C, 475 F, Gas 9 for about 15 minutes, or until browned and very crisp. Serve at once. Make gravy in the microwave following the instructions on page 85.

Cooking Duck Portions The timing per 450g/1lb for portions is the same as for a whole bird. The portions can be browned in one of two ways: by browning the skin in a very hot frying pan before cooking in the microwave, or by browning the skin under the grill after cooking. If the portions are to be casseroled, then the best solution is to remove the skin and fat before cooking.

The following timings are a guide to cooking portions on full:

1 quarter	− 4–6 minutes
2 quarters	− 7–9 minutes
3 quarters	− 12–15 minutes
4 quarters	− 17–20 minutes

Arrange thin bone ends together towards the middle of the dish and turn the portions halfway through cooking. Season after cooking.

Cooking Boneless, Skinned Duck Breasts Best cooked with at least a little liquid. Arrange in a dish and sprinkle over 150ml/¼ pint fresh orange juice, stock or red or white wine. Add a couple of bay leaves, tucking them under the meat, and freshly ground black pepper. Cover and cook on full for the following times, turning the pieces of meat over halfway through cooking and rearranging them as necessary.

1 portion	– 4–6 minutes
2 portions	– 6–8 minutes
3 portions	– 12–15 minutes
4 portions	– 16–18 minutes

The exact time depends on the size of the fillets. The cooking juices can be thickened with a little arrowroot or cornflour blended with cold water and heated for 30–60 seconds to boil. Stir in 1–2 tablespoons redcurrant or apple jelly, or orange marmalade before thickening.

DUMPLINGS

Suet pastry dumplings can be cooked in the microwave with excellent results. They should be placed on top of a moist dish – a fish, poultry or bacon casserole which has been cooked in the microwave, or a stew which has been cooked conventionally, frozen, then reheated in the microwave. Make the pastry by mixing 50g/2oz suet into 100g/4oz self-raising flour. Add seasoning, 3 tablespoons chopped parsley and mix to a soft dough with 50ml/2fl oz water. From this, shape six dumplings. Place them on the surface of the casserole and cook on full for 3½–4½ minutes. Alternatively the dumplings can be cooked on their own, in a greased dish with 2 tablespoons water added. Cover the dish and cook for 3–4 minutes on full, or until the dumplings are risen, fluffy and just firm.

DYEING FABRIC

The microwave can be used for dyeing fabric (although the lengths have to be manageable – scarves, shirts and tops are suitable) to achieve a tie-dyed effect, or uneven swirls of colour. Dylon recommend the use of their Natural Fabric Dye but the method is not suitable for wool or viscose and other synthetic fabrics. It can be used for cottons, polyester-cotton, linen – or silk!

> *Remember that you must not put any garments that have metal clips or fasteners into the microwave.*

The dye is dissolved in 600ml/1 pint cold water in a suitable, large, microwave-proof bowl. The fabric is immersed in the dye and covered before being 'cooked' on full for 4 minutes. The fabric is then rinsed until the water runs clear. It makes a change from using the microwave for cooking!

EGGS

The quality of eggs cooked in the microwave depends on their preparation. Scrambled eggs are delicious if they are whisked frequently during cooking; eggs cooked in individual dishes are best if other ingredients are added – diced vegetables, spinach or tomatoes and cheese; they can also be cooked plain, either by 'poaching' with a little water or by cooking in individual buttered dishes. The acceptability of eggs cooked plain depends on taste – if you are fussy about eggs, favouring the whites firm and the yolks runny, then you may well dislike microwave-cooked eggs as the yolk has a tendency to cook quickly while the white can still be slightly soft. Never try to cook eggs whole, in their shells, in the microwave as they will explode and spatter all over the oven.

> *When cooking eggs which are not whisked*

> *always prick the yolk very lightly with a cocktail stick – it is covered by a fine membrane and if this is not pricked then the yolk may burst and spatter during cooking.*

Scrambled Eggs When scrambling eggs in the microwave, add just a little milk and a good knob of butter. For dieters or those on a low-fat diet, then simply cook the eggs plain. Add seasoning before cooking. The secret of success is to whisk the eggs well before cooking, then to whisk them frequently as they set. Watch them cooking – when you see a rim of set egg round the side of the basin, then remove from the microwave and whisk well to break and mix in the set egg. The eggs are cooked when they are just too soft – by the time they are stirred and served they should be perfect. These timings are only a guide, as the starting temperature of the eggs makes a difference – those from the refrigerator take longer to cook than those at room temperature. Use full power and do not cover the dish.

2 eggs + 1 tablespoon milk	1–1½ minutes
4 eggs + 2 tablespoons milk	3–4 minutes
6 eggs + 3 tablespoons milk	5½–6½ minutes

Plain Cooked Eggs Crack the eggs into buttered individual dishes or into a special microwave-proof bun dish. Top each with a dot of butter and cover (saucers or microwave-proof cling film can be used). The following times are a guide – adjust slightly to suit your own taste. Cook on full.

1 egg – ½–1 minute	
2 eggs – 1–1½ minutes	
3 eggs – 1½–1¾ minutes	
4 eggs – 1¾–2 minutes	

Poached Eggs Again, the acceptability depends on individual preference. Place 2 tablespoons boiling water from the kettle in each individual dish, adding a few drops of vinegar. Crack an egg into each, prick the yolk lightly with a cocktail stick and cook as above. Drain before serving.

FENNEL

Fennel has a delicate aniseed flavour and a texture similar to celery. For best results the bulbs should be trimmed and sliced for microwave cooking. Alternatively, the chopped vegetable can be used in casserole-type dishes, particularly with chicken. Cook chopped fennel with rice and onions to make a delicious and unusual risotto.

Braised Fennel Finely chop 1 onion and cook it with a knob of butter on full for 3 minutes. Add 450g/1lb trimmed and sliced fennel, a little lemon juice, 4 tablespoons chicken stock, white wine or water and some freshly ground black pepper. Cover and cook on full for 8–10 minutes, stirring halfway through cooking. Blend 2 teaspoons cornflour to a paste with a little cold water, stir into the fennel and cook for 1–2 minutes, until the juices are thickened. Season to taste with salt before serving.

FIGS, DRIED

Dried figs can be cooked in the microwave without having to be pre-soaked. Place 12 figs in a large dish and pour in 300ml/½ pint medium-sweet cider, apple juice or fresh orange juice. Add a cinnamon stick and 2–4 tablespoons sugar (to taste). Cover and cook on full for 8–10 minutes. Leave the figs to stand for 5 minutes before serving. If you like, add 2 cloves and 4 green cardamom pods for a spicy result. The figs are also good cold.

FISH
See also Herring, Kippers, Mackerel, Mullet, Plaice, Salmon and Trout.

Tender, light fish cooks very well in the microwave to give moist, full-flavoured results. Depending on the type of fish, it can be cooked whole, in steaks or cutlets, in fillets or cut into chunks. For use in pies, fish cakes or other recipes which call for cooked fish, it can be cooked very simply without any additional ingredients. Alternatively fillets or steaks can be dotted with butter or margarine, moistened with lemon juice, wine or water and sprinkled with fresh herbs before cooking. Steaks, individual portions, fillets or chunks can also be cooked in a sauce. Whichever method is used, the fish should not be seasoned with salt before cooking and the dish should be covered during cooking.

> *When cooking several portions of fish, they should be checked halfway through and turned or rearranged to ensure even results. Thicker parts of the fillet, or the thick end of a steak, should be placed towards the outside of the dish, with thinner areas in the centre. When cooking two or more large fish fillets, arrange them in a dish with head ends next to tail ends and tuck the thin tail ends underneath the head ends of other fillets to prevent them from overcooking. Chunks of fish should be placed in the dish as far apart as possible and they should be rearranged and turned halfway through cooking.*

Defrosting Fish Use defrost setting or the power setting recommended by the manufacturer for defrosting. Fish should be covered during defrosting and it should be rearranged at least once. Fillets which are frozen in a block should be separated as soon as possible. Thick parts should be arranged towards the outside of the dish and thin areas towards the middle as for cooking. The fish is ready for cooking when it is still slightly icy. The following timings are a guide; leave the fish to stand for about 5 minutes before cooking.

Fillets (for example cod, coley, haddock, plaice, whiting etc)	100g/4oz	2–4 minutes
	225g/8oz	5–7 minutes
	450g/1lb	8–10 minutes
Steaks and Cutlets (for example cod, hake, salmon etc. Exact times depend on the thickness of the steaks or cutlets. Select evenly sized and shaped portions for best results.)	2 medium	4–8 minutes
	3 medium	5–9 minutes
	4 medium	7–12 minutes

Cooking Fish The following is a guide to cooking times using full power. When cooked the fish should flake easily but still be very slightly translucent at the base of the flakes or towards the centre of the cutlet or steak. By the time the fish is removed from the microwave and served the residual heat will have completed the cooking process.

Fillets

100g/4oz – 1½–2½ minutes
225g/8oz – 4–6 minutes
450g/1lb – 7–10 minutes

Cutlets or Steaks

1 medium – 2–4 minutes
2 medium – 4–6 minutes
3 medium – 5–7 minutes
4 medium – 8–10 minutes

Cooking Frozen Preformed Fish Steaks The small oblong blocks of frozen fish can be cooked straight from frozen. They are useful for making pies, or for adding to a cheese or mushroom sauce to be served with mashed potatoes, rice or pasta. If the fish is to be added to a sauce it should be three-quarters cooked, then cut into chunks and cooked briefly in the sauce before serving. The following times are a guide to cooking on full, in a covered dish. Turn and rearrange the blocks of fish frequently during cooking.

1 frozen steak – 2–3 minutes
2 frozen steaks – 4–6 minutes
3 frozen steaks – 7–9 minutes
4 frozen steaks – 9–11 minutes

FISH CAKES

These will not become crisp when cooked in the microwave and the result is inferior. They are best cooked by conventional methods (frying, grilling or baking) although you can achieve an acceptable result using a microwave browning dish. To cook fish cakes in a browning dish, heat the dish according to the manufacturer's instructions, add a little butter or oil and place the cakes in the dish. Cook for half the time, turn the cakes and cook for the remaining time.

2 cakes – 2–3 minutes
4 cakes – 4–6 minutes

For frozen fish cakes allow an extra 1–2 minutes.

FISH FINGERS

These do not become crisp and they are best cooked by conventional methods.

FLANS, SAVOURY

Savoury flans consisting of a pastry case with a set filling based on eggs and milk can be part-cooked in the microwave to give acceptable results. The pastry case should be cooked conventionally, and allowed to cool, then the filling can be set in the microwave. The advantage of this is that an empty pastry case can be cooked when the oven is hot then set aside in the refrigerator for up to three days before filling. Cook chopped onion, bacon or similar raw ingredients before placing them in the flan. Allow 3 minutes on full for 1 medium chopped onion, cooking it in a covered dish with a knob of butter or 1 tablespoon oil. Diced cooked ham, flaked tuna fish, defrosted frozen peas, sliced mushrooms and grated cheese are all suitable ingredients for filling the flan. To fill a 20–23cm/8–9in flan, heat 300ml/½ pint milk on full for 2 minutes, until hot but not boiling. Beat 3 eggs with seasoning to taste, then slowly beat in the hot milk. Cook on full for 30–60 seconds until just beginning to thicken. Pour the egg mixture into the pastry case and cook on medium for 9–12 minutes, until the mixture is set. Leave to stand for 5 minutes.

Reheating Chilled Cooked Flans Chilled cooked flans can be speedily reheated in the microwave, although the pastry case does become rather soggy.

1 medium slice – ½–1 minute
2 medium slices – 1–1½ minutes
half a flan – 2–3 minutes
whole flan (about 20cm/8in) – 3–4 minutes

Defrosting Flans Defrost and reheat flans in one operation. Slices can be defrosted and reheated on full but whole flans should be defrosted and reheated on medium to prevent some areas from overheating before other parts are defrosted.

> *Cover the top with absorbent kitchen paper to absorb excess moisture which tends to seep from the flan as it defrosts.*

1 medium slice – 1½–2 minutes
2 medium slices – 2–3 minutes
whole flan (20cm/8in) – 8–10 minutes (allow the flan to stand for 3 minutes before serving)

FLAPJACKS

A small batch of oaty flapjacks can be cooked successfully in the microwave. Cook 50g/2oz butter and 50g/2oz golden syrup on full for 1–2 minutes, until the butter has melted. Stir in 100g/4oz rolled oats, 50g/2oz roughly chopped raisins, 2 tablespoons plain flour and ½ teaspoon ground mixed spice. Mix thoroughly then press into a greased oblong dish measuring about 13 × 19cm/5 × 7½in. Cook on full for 2–4 minutes, then leave until just warm. Cut into fingers and leave to cool. Lift from the dish when completely cold.

FOIL

Always read and follow the microwave manufacturer's advice on the use of foil in your microwave. As a general rule do not use foil except when cut into small pieces to shield small areas of food that are likely to overcook; make sure the foil is shiny side outwards to reflect the microwaves off the area. Some microwave manufacturers suggest that small, shallow foil containers which are well filled with food can be used, but unless this is clearly explained in the instruction book then remove all convenience foods from foil containers before cooking in the microwave.

FONDUE
See Cheese Fondue, page 37.

FRANKFURTERS
These can be heated quickly and successfully in the microwave. If they are packed in a boilable bag, then pierce the bag and place it in a dish. Alternatively, place the loose frankfurters in a dish, cover and cook on full.

1 – about 30 seconds	
2 – about 1–1¾ minutes	
3 – about 1½–2 minutes	
4 – about 2–3 minutes	
6 – about 4–5 minutes	
8 – about 6–7 minutes	

If more than four frankfurters are cooked they should be rearranged halfway through cooking. Serve them hot in split rolls. If you like onions in your hot dogs, then chop 1 large onion and cook it with a knob of butter in a small covered basin on full for 3–5 minutes before cooking the frankfurters.

FRENCH BEANS
See Beans, page 19.

FRUIT, DRIED
See also Figs, Dried, page 73.
 Dried fruit can be cooked in the microwave

without having to be pre-soaked. The fruit should be placed in a fairly deep dish, basin or bowl and covered well with liquid – water, fruit juice or cider can be used. Cover the dish and cook on full, pressing the fruit into the liquid once or twice during cooking. Stir to rearrange the fruit. When it is just tender, leave it to stand for 5 minutes before serving. Alternatively, the cooked fruit can be allowed to cool completely before serving. For 225g/8oz fruit you will need about 450ml/¾ pint liquid and it should be cooked for 14–16 minutes. If the fruit is cooked in water, then add a little sugar to taste after cooking.

FRUIT, FRESH
See Apples, Blackberries etc.

Fresh fruit cooks well in the microwave. Depending on the type of fruit it can be lightly cooked until just tender or well cooked so that it can be puréed. The fruit should be prepared according to its type as for conventional cooking methods. Fruits cooked in their skin should be pierced, for example whole apples should be scored round the middle to prevent them bursting.

G

GAMMON
Gammon is a tender meat which can be cooked successfully in the microwave. Best results are obtained with steaks or cubed gammon, although joints can also be cooked in the microwave.
Defrosting Gammon Steaks Use defrost power; if the steaks are frozen together, then separate them as

soon as possible during defrosting. They should be turned once or twice during defrosting and the dish should be covered. The following timing guide is for steaks weighing between 100–175g/4–6oz each.

1 – 2–3 minutes	
2 – 4–5 minutes	
3 – 6–7 minutes	
4 – 8–9 minutes	

Cooking Gammon Steaks Trim off the rind and excess fat, then snip the remaining fat to prevent the steaks from curling. The steaks should be arranged on a large flat dish – a flan dish is suitable – overlapping them as little as possible. Turn and rearrange the steaks once or twice during cooking. Cover with absorbent kitchen paper. Alternatively, sprinkle the steaks with about 150ml/¼ pint medium-sweet cider or apple juice and cover the dish with a lid or upturned plate. The following times are a guide for cooking medium steaks (weighing about 100–175g/4–6oz) on full. For best results, the steaks should not be too thin and they should be fairly small and neat.

1 – 2–3 minutes	
2 – 5–7 minutes	
3 – 6–8 minutes	
4 – 7–10 minutes	

Gammon Stew Cut 450g/1lb lean gammon into chunks. Toss 2 sliced carrots and 1 chopped onion with 2 tablespoons oil, cover and cook on full for 5 minutes. Add a bay leaf, the gammon and 100g/4oz sliced mushrooms. Stir in 2 tablespoons flour and pour in 300ml/½ pint stock or medium-sweet cider. Season with pepper, cover and cook on full for

10–12 minutes, stirring twice, until the carrots and gammon are cooked. Sprinkle with plenty of chopped fresh parsley and stir well before serving.

Gammon Joints For best results cook a gammon joint by traditional boiling or baking. Large joints take a long time to cook through in the microwave and the outside tends to become dry before the middle is cooked. However a small joint can be cooked in the microwave with reasonable success. First weigh the joint and calculate the cooking time at about 7–8 minutes per 450g/1lb on full. Soak the gammon in cold water for several hours, drain it and make sure it is tied securely into a neat shape. Place in a large dish and add 150ml/¼ pint cold water, apple juice or medium-sweet cider. The joint can be studded with cloves and a quartered onion and bay leaf added to the dish for extra flavour. Cover the dish and cook for half the calculated time. Leave the joint to stand for 15 minutes, then turn it and cook for the remaining time. Allow to stand for 15 minutes before piercing the centre of the joint to make sure that it is cooked through.

GARLIC BREAD

The microwave is useful for speedily heating some buttery garlic bread. The result is not crisp and crunchy as expected of bread heated in the conventional oven but it is an acceptable alternative considering the speed and the fact that you do not have to preheat the oven. For a short French stick, or ½ long French loaf, beat 1 or 2 crushed garlic cloves into 75g/3oz butter. Cut the bread into thick slices and spread them with garlic butter. Press the slices together into two long pieces, place on a plate and cover with a double thickness of absorbent kitchen paper. Heat on full for about 1 minute. The butter melts very quickly and the garlic bread can

become very hot – so take care!
Herb Bread Instead of garlic, beat plenty of chopped fresh herbs into the butter – for example parsley, thyme, tarragon, marjoram, savoury and chives.

GELATINE

Powdered gelatine can be dissolved successfully in the microwave but take great care not to overheat the liquid and boil the gelatine. Sprinkle 3 teaspoons gelatine over 3–4 tablespoons cold water in a basin and leave for 2 minutes. Heat on full for 30–45 seconds, then stir until the gelatine has dissolved completely.

GINGERBREAD

Small quantities of gingerbread can be cooked successfully in the microwave. Heat 50g/2oz margarine with 50g/2oz black treacle and 50g/2oz soft brown sugar on full for 1–2 minutes, until melted. Add the melted mixture to 100g/4oz self-raising flour mixed with 1 tablespoon ground ginger. Stir in ¼ teaspoon bicarbonate of soda, dissolved in 1 tablespoon cold milk, and a beaten egg. When all the ingredients are thoroughly combined pour the mixture into a greased 900ml/1½ pint dish – for best results use a ring dish. Cook on full for 2–4 minutes, until the gingerbread is firm to the touch but slightly sticky on top. Leave in the dish for 10 minutes before turning out to cool. Wrap closely in foil or cling film when still warm to retain the moisture. Leave for 24 hours before slicing.

GLASSWARE

Glassware can be used for heating or cooking in the microwave. Do not use cut glass as this can cause sparking. Inexpensive tumblers and wine glasses can be used for heating drinks.

Ovenproof glass dishes are ideal for cooking food in the microwave – casseroles, flan dishes, loaf dishes and measuring jugs are all useful. Similarly mixing bowls and basins of this type make useful containers for soups and sauces.

GNOCCHI

Gnocchi are small 'dumplings' which can be made from either potato or semolina. The microwave is useful for preparing the semolina version. Pour 600ml/1 pint boiling water into a mixing bowl or large casserole. Whisk in 200g/7oz semolina, then cook it on full for 3–5 minutes until thickened. Beat the semolina thoroughly. Add 8 tablespoons freshly grated Parmesan cheese, 50g/2oz butter and seasoning and beat the mixture thoroughly. Lastly beat in a large egg. Spread the mixture in a shallow tin and leave it to cool. Chill the gnocchi for several hours or overnight. Cut it into squares, overlap them in a buttered dish, cover and cook on full for 9–11 minutes. Sprinkle with plenty of chopped parsley or fresh basil, a little oregano and a pinch of thyme. Top with an even layer of diced mozzarella or grated mild cheese and brown under the grill before serving with a tomato sauce.

GOOSEBERRIES

These cook very well in the microwave. Top and tail the fruit, then add sugar to taste and cover the dish. The gooseberries tend to burst during cooking so it is important to cover the dish. Cook on full for the following times:

450g/1lb – 4–6 minutes	
675g/1½lb – 8–10 minutes	

Frozen Gooseberries

450g/1lb – 7–9 minutes	

675g/1½lb – 12–14 minutes

> **Note** *Free-flow frozen fruit will cook more quickly than fruit which is frozen in a block. Break up a block of fruit as soon as possible during cooking.*

GRAPEFRUIT

Hot fresh grapefruit makes a light and inexpensive starter. Serve it plain, topped with brown sugar, or sprinkle with a little ginger wine, sweet vermouth or orange liqueur before heating. Instead of brown sugar you may like to sweeten the fruit with honey. Halve the grapefruit, loosen the segments, then stand the halves as far apart as possible on a large plate. Support them with crumpled absorbent kitchen paper if necessary. Heat on full for the following times:

2 halves – about 1 minute

4 halves – 2–3 minutes

GRAVY

The microwave is useful for making gravy. For the best flavour use all the juices from roasting meat, scraping the roasting pan well and rinsing it with a little boiling water to obtain the maximum flavour. A large basin or 1.15 litre/2 pint measuring jug is ideal for making gravy in the microwave. Place 40g/1½oz plain flour in the basin. Scrape all the cooking juices from the roasting pan and mix with 600ml/1 pint boiling water. Slowly stir this into the flour and whisk thoroughly until smooth. Add seasoning and cook on full for 10 minutes, whisking twice to make a smooth thickened gravy. If there is not enough flavour from the roast, then add a crumbled stock cube to the gravy. A little tomato purée and a dash of Worcestershire sauce can also be added to enliven a plain gravy. If you like, whisk in a little gravy browning halfway through cooking.

HADDOCK
See Fish, page 74.

Both white and smoked haddock fillets cook well in the microwave. Fresh haddock steaks and cutlets are sometimes available. Follow cooking times and instructions for fish fillets, cutlets and steaks.

HAKE
See Fish, page 74.

A firm white fish which cooks well in the microwave, the steaks are small and neat. Follow instructions for fish cutlets and steaks.

HALIBUT
See Fish, page 74.

A firm, meaty fish cut into fillets or thin, boat-shaped steaks. Follow instructions for fish fillets, cutlets and steaks.

HALOGEN MICROWAVE COOKER
See Combination Microwave Cooking, page 50.

This type of cooker provides the facility for basic microwave cooking and, in addition, it is fitted with halogen filaments which produce radiant heat similar to that of a conventional grill. The appliances can be used in a similar way to a combination microwave but the result is more like using a combination of grilling and microwaves rather than baking and microwaves. The filaments which provide the conventional heat are located in the top and sides of the oven so they give all round heat. The conventional heat can be used alone, either both sides and top or top only for grilling food. The heat can also be used in combination with the microwaves and again this can be controlled to heat both sides and top or the top filament only. Follow the manufacturer's instructions closely for timings, the advantages being that the food browns and crisps as for conventional cooking. Roasts, pastry and baked items can be cooked with success in this type of oven.

HAMBURGERS
See Beef, page 20.

HEART
Unlike most other offal, heart requires lengthy, moist cooking for best results, and is therefore better suited to traditional cooking methods.

HERBS
Use the microwave to dry herbs. Thoroughly wash and dry freshly picked herbs, selecting the best sprigs and leaves. Spread out on a double thickness of absorbent kitchen paper on a large plate. Cover with a double-thick piece of absorbent kitchen paper and cook on full for 2 minutes. Rearrange the herbs and cover with fresh paper, then continue to cook for 30–60 second spurts until the herbs are just dry. Uncover the sprigs and leave them to cool when they should be completely dried. Crumble them into an airtight container for storage. The exact timing depends on the type of herbs – 25g/1oz parsley takes

about 4 minutes to dry. Check the herbs frequently during drying.

> Never set the timer for several minutes and leave the microwave unattended when cooking small quantities such as here.

HERRING

Herring cook very well in the microwave. Clean and gut the fish and remove the heads. Make two or three slashes into each side of the skin, then arrange the fish in a dish head to tail. Cover and cook on full power, rearranging and turning the fish halfway through cooking.

2 – 2–3 minutes	
4 – 4–6 minutes	

Rolled Herring Fillets Season herring fillets with black pepper and flavour with grated lemon rind. Spread with a little mustard or creamed horseradish if you like. Roll up and secure with wooden cocktail sticks. Arrange the rolls round the edge of a dish and add a couple of bay leaves. Sprinkle with 4 tablespoons water, cover and cook on full.

4 rolls (from 2 whole fish) – 3–4 minutes
8 rolls (from 4 whole fish) – 7–9 minutes

HOLLANDAISE SAUCE

This sauce is prepared with ease in the microwave. Use a large basin for best results. Heat 2 tablespoons lemon juice and 1 tablespoon water on full for 1–2 minutes, until boiling and slightly reduced. Remove, add seasoning to taste and immediately whisk in 2 large egg yolks. In a separate jug heat 100g/4oz butter on full for 2–3 minutes until it is melted and very hot. Whisking all the time, slowly pour the butter in a thin trickle on to the yolks. When all the butter has been incorporated heat the sauce for 30 seconds on full and serve immediately.

Alternatively, place the yolks, hot lemon juice and seasoning in a blender and process until pale and thoroughly combined. Heat the butter as above, allowing an extra 30 seconds so that it is very hot. With the blender running, slowly trickle the very hot butter on to the yolks. If the butter is hot enough the sauce will not require further cooking and it can be served at once.

HONEY

If a pot of honey has started to crystallise, then heat it in the microwave for a few seconds and stir lightly to dissolve the crystals. Remember to remove the lid and any other metal on the pot before putting it in the microwave. If there is just a small amount of honey in the pot, then 5–10 seconds on full may be long enough to dissolve the crystals.

Honey Toddy Place 2 teaspoons honey, the juice of ½ lemon and a dash of whisky in a mug. Top up with cold water and heat on full for 45–60 seconds, until thoroughly warmed. Stir well before drinking – great to ward off the first signs of a cold or heart-warming after a chilly winter walk!

I

ICE CREAM

The microwave can be used to make a custard sauce which forms the base for a creamy homemade ice cream. It is also useful for softening ice cream which is too hard to be scooped out of its container; it is best to use medium setting for this and about 30 seconds should be enough to soften the ice cream sufficiently.

Homemade Ice Cream Prepare a custard sauce using egg yolks, following the instructions on page 62. Cover the surface of the sauce with a piece of damp greaseproof paper and leave it until cold. Whip 300ml/½ pint double cream with 50g/2oz icing sugar and ½ teaspoon vanilla essence. Fold the cream into the custard. Whisk 2 egg whites until stiff, then fold them into the custard. Turn it into a container and freeze. Whisk thoroughly when half frozen, then whisk twice more during freezing to make a smooth ice cream which is free of crystals. Freeze until firm before serving.

J

JAM
Although the microwave is useful for making a small quantity of jam it is not realistic to suggest that it can be used for preserving in the traditional sense. To boil large quantities of any sweet preserve you need a large container and the majority of bowls which will fit into the microwave are simply too small to allow the preserve to bubble up. However, the microwave can be used to make a small quantity.

Strawberry and Apple Jam Wash and roughly chop 1 small cooking apple. Place it in a basin and add 6 tablespoons water. Cover and cook on full for 8–10 minutes, until the apple is reduced to a pulp. Press it through a fine sieve and place the purée in a bowl. Add the juice of ½ lemon and 225g/8oz hulled strawberries. Cover and cook on full for 3–5 minutes, until the strawberries are soft. Stir in 225g/8oz sugar and cook on full for 2 minutes. Stir again to make sure the sugar has dissolved completely. When the sugar has dissolved, replace the bowl in the microwave and cook on full until you can see that all the preserve is bubbling and boiling evenly – about 2 minutes. Continue to cook for 2 minutes, then remove the jam from the oven and test it for setting by placing a small spoonful on a very cold saucer. As it cools the jam should form a skin which will wrinkle when pushed with a finger. If it does not set, return the jam to the microwave and cook for a further 1 minute on full. Continue cooking the jam in this way until setting point is reached. This should take about 10 minutes at most. This quantity will yield two pots.

JELLY TABLETS
Dissolve jelly tablets with a little water in a basin in the microwave, then make up the quantity according to the manufacturer's instructions by adding ice cold water. The jelly will set very quickly! Break the tablet into squares and place in a basin with 5 tablespoons water. Heat on full for 1–2 minutes, then stir until the jelly has dissolved completely.

KIDNEYS
Tender lamb's kidneys cook well in the microwave but they must be cooked in a covered dish as they

tend to spit. When ready they should be very slightly pink in the centre.

Kidneys with Bacon Place 1 finely chopped onion in a dish with 100g/4oz chopped smoked bacon and a knob of butter. Cover and cook on full for 5 minutes. Halve and core 450g/1lb lamb's kidneys and add them to the dish, stirring well. Stir in 2 tablespoons dry sherry or stock, cover and cook on full for 3–5 minutes, stirring once, until the kidneys are almost cooked. Stir in 100g/4oz thinly sliced mushrooms and cook for a further 1–2 minutes. Season to taste before serving. Good on hot buttered toast; alternatively spoon the kidneys over cooked rice or pasta and top with a little soured cream or yogurt.

Note For a tasty breakfast dish, omit the onion but use double the quantity of bacon and cook it for 3–4 minutes before adding the kidneys. Cover the dish and cook the kidneys as above, omitting the sherry or stock, for 3–5 minutes. Serve with fried eggs, crisply grilled sausages and hot toast.

KIPPERS

These require the minimum cooking and can be prepared very well in the microwave. Place in a covered dish, or use a roasting bag closed with a microwave-proof tie. Cook on full for the following times, rearranging the fish halfway through if cooking two or more.

1 – about 1 minute
2 – 1½–3 minutes
3 – 2½–4 minutes
4 – 4–6 minutes

Frozen Boil-in-the-bag Kippers Pierce the bag and lay it on a plate or dish. Cook on full for 4–6 minutes. Leave for 1–2 minutes before snipping the bag. Look out for the manufacturer's instructions on the packet – many brands of frozen food have been specifically tested for microwave reheating and precise instructions are provided.

KOHLRABI
A vegetable which is similar in flavour to swede or turnip but slightly more delicate.It should be peeled and cut up for cooking. Cut the vegetable into matchstick strips or small cubes and place in a dish with 3 tablespoons water. Cover and cook on full power, allowing about 9–11 minutes for 450g/1lb. Stir to rearrange the vegetable halfway through cooking, then drain away any cooking liquid and serve topped with butter and pepper. The vegetable can also be mashed to a purée and creamed with butter, pepper and a little soured cream.

KUMQUATS
These tiny oval oranges can be poached in the microwave to serve as part of a dessert. The poached kumquats can be cooled and added to a fruit salad or they can be used to liven up simple puddings such as stewed apples, apple crumble or even apple pie! Alternatively, the kumquats can be served in their syrup as a topping for a steamed sponge pudding (spoon the fruit over the cooked pudding just before it is served), as an unusual filling for pancakes (cooked conventionally), as a topping for ice cream or to complement plain cooked bananas.

Wash and slice 225g/8oz kumquats, making the slices fairly thick and removing the pips. Place in a dish with 150ml/¼ pint water, a cinnamon stick and 2 cloves. Cover and cook on full for 5–7 minutes, stirring halfway through cooking, until the fruit is tender. Discard the spices and add 50g/2oz sugar to the fruit, then stir well and cook, uncovered, for a further 1–2 minutes, or until the sugar has dissolved completely.

Savoury Kumquat Sauce To serve with gammon steaks, pork chops, cooked ham, roast duck or chicken, or other similar main dishes that are complemented by the orange flavour. Wash and thinly slice 75g/3oz kumquats, removing all the pips. Place them in a basin and add a bay leaf, a sprig each of parsley and thyme, and 300ml/½ pint stock. Cover and cook on full for 5–7 minutes, until the kumquats are tender and the liquid well flavoured with herbs. Leave to stand for 10 minutes. Meanwhile, cook 2 tablespoons finely chopped onion with 3 tablespoons dry sherry in a covered basin on full for 3 minutes. Stir in 4 tablespoons redcurrant jelly. Blend 1 tablespoon cornflour with a little cold water. Remove the herbs from the kumquats, then stir them and their cooking stock into the onion mixture. Stir in the cornflour and cook on full for about 2–3 minutes, until the sauce is boiling and thickened. Serve hot.

LAMB
Tender cuts of lamb – for example leg, shoulder, fillet and chops – can be cooked in the microwave but, like all meat, the best results are obtained by traditional or combination microwave cooking. This said, a joint of lamb which is part cooked in the microwave, then finished off in a hot conventional oven is deliciously succulent and moist, and the cooking time is greatly reduced.

Defrosting Lamb Unwrap the meat and place it in a dish, arranging chops or cutlets as far apart as possible. Cover and defrost on defrost setting, turning small portions halfway through. Turn joints at least three times during cooking. Check to make sure that the thin parts of the joint do not begin to cook before other areas are softened. If necessary, protect thin areas with small pieces of foil. Calculate the defrosting time by weight and allow small portions to stand for 10–15 minutes before cooking. Joints should be allowed to stand for about 30 minutes before cooking.

Chops, cutlets or steaks	per 450g/1lb	6–8 minutes
Joints	per 450g/1lb	5–7 minutes

At the end of the calculated time the meat should be softened but still icy in the middle. Drain and dry the meat on absorbent kitchen paper before cooking.

Cooking Lamb Chops or Cutlets A browning dish can be used to lightly brown the chops (follow the manufacturer's instructions for heating the dish), or they can be cooked in wine, stock or a sauce, in which case the fact that the meat is not browned is not as noticeable. Trim chops of excess fat before cooking and arrange them as far apart as possible on a shallow dish. Cover with absorbent kitchen paper. If they are cooked in a sauce, then arrange the chops in a covered dish. Cook on full and rearrange the chops halfway through cooking.

1 – 2–4 minutes
2 – 5–7 minutes
3 – 6–8 minutes
4 – 8–10 minutes

Cooking Lamb Joints Boned joints, tied into a neat

shape, give best results but meat on the bone can be cooked successfully.

> *Any thin areas of meat may need protecting by covering with small pieces of foil to prevent them from overcooking.*

Weigh the joint and calculate the cooking time, including any stuffing in the weight, then season it with pepper and sprinkle with rosemary or other fresh herbs. Brush the outside of the meat with a little oil and cook it in a covered dish. Allow 7–9 minutes per 450g/1lb on full, depending on how well cooked you like your lamb. Turn the joint over at least twice during cooking and allow the meat to stand for 15 minutes before checking whether it is cooked to your liking. To part-microwave the meat allow about 5–7 minutes per 450g/1lb, then finish the roast in the conventional oven at 200–220 C/ 400–425 F/gas 6–7 for about 20–30 minutes.

Cooking Minced Lamb This cooks well in the microwave and can be shaped into burgers, used to make a meat sauce which is excellent with cooked chick peas or buckwheat, or it can be used as a base for a cottage pie. Follow instructions and timings given for minced beef, page 22.

Lamb Stew Traditional stewing cuts of lamb do not cook well in the microwave and they should be cooked by conventional, long, slow methods.

Lamb Casseroles Tender cuts of lamb can be used to make casseroles in the microwave; leg or fillet are suitable. Trim all fat and any gristle from the meat, then cut it across the grain into small, bite-sized slices that are quite thin. This method of cutting gives the most tender results. As a basic guide, place 1 chopped onion in a dish with 1 tablespoon oil, cover and cook on full for 3 minutes. Add 450g/1lb prepared lamb and stir in 2 tablespoons flour. Add

300ml/½ pint red wine or stock, 1 tablespoon tomato purée, 1 bay leaf, a little salt and plenty of pepper, 100g/4oz thinly sliced carrots and 100g/4oz sliced button mushrooms. Mix well, cover and cook on full for 25–30 minutes, stirring twice during cooking, until the lamb is tender.

LASAGNE

Sheets of dried lasagne are best boiled by conventional methods. Their size and shape, and the fact that the sheets stick together very easily during cooking, means that to cook the sheets of lasagne successfully in the microwave is more trouble than it is worth.

Lasagne al Forno Although you are better advised to use the conventional hob to cook the sheets of pasta, the microwave is a great help when preparing dishes of sauce layered with pasta. Cook the pasta first or buy the no-need-to-cook pasta. Prepare a Bolognese sauce (see page 23) and a cheese sauce (see page 20). Select a dish which will fit in the microwave – it does not have to be oblong as the pasta can be trimmed to fit.

> *Make sure that the dish is large enough to hold all the sauce and do not overfill it as the sauces may boil over during cooking.*

Butter the dish and layer the pasta, meat and cheese sauces into it. Reserve a little cheese sauce for the top and end with a layer of pasta. Spread the reserved cheese sauce over the lasagne, then cook on full power. If using boiled pasta, cook for 3–5 minutes, until the lasagne is bubbling hot, and brown the top under the grill if you like. If the no-need-to-cook pasta is used, then cook the lasagne on medium for 20–25 minutes, until the pasta is tender.

Ratatouille Lasagne Ratatouille makes delicious

lasagne. Prepare the ratatouille (see page 130) and a cheese sauce (see page 20). Layer and cook as for Lasagne al Forno, above.

LEEKS
These cook very well in the microwave, either sliced, cut into lengths or whole if the vegetables are small. Trim, prepare and thoroughly wash the leeks, then place in a dish with 3 tablespoons water. Cover and cook on full. Whole leeks can be cooked in a roasting bag, closed with a microwave-proof tie. Stir or rearrange the leeks halfway through cooking.

225g/8oz	sliced	4–6 minutes
450g/1lb	sliced	8–10 minutes
450g/1lb	whole	7–10 minutes
225g/8oz	frozen sliced	5–7 minutes
450g/1lb	frozen sliced	10–12 minutes

Note There is no need to add water to frozen leeks.

LEMONS
To extract the maximum juice from a lemon heat the whole fruit in the microwave on full for 30–45 seconds before halving and squeezing it.

LEMON CURD
In a bowl which is suitable for microwave cooking, beat 3 large eggs with the grated rind of 3 lemons. In a separate basin mix 100g/4oz butter, the juice squeezed from the lemons and 350g/12oz caster sugar; cook on full for 5–6 minutes, or until the butter has melted and all the ingredients are hot. Stir well, then slowly pour the butter and sugar mixture on to the eggs, whisking continuously. Cook the curd on full for 6 minutes, whisking well every 2 minutes. When cooked the curd should be thickened

enough to coat the back of a spoon: cook for 1 minute, whisk well and continue cooking for spurts of 1 minute until the curd is thickened. The total time should be between 8–10 minutes but this varies with individual ovens and depends also on the starting temperature of the eggs. Do not overcook the lemon curd or it will curdle. It is important to whisk the curd every minute to prevent some parts from overcooking. The result is excellent!

Strain the curd into two 450g/1lb warmed pots and cover immediately with waxed discs. Top when quite cold with cellophane covers or lids and label the pots. The curd will keep for up to one month if stored in the refrigerator.

LENTILS
These cook very well in the microwave and can be turned into a wide variety of delicious dishes or served simply as an accompaniment.

The important point to remember is to ensure the lentils are in a dish large enough to allow them to boil up without spilling over. If you do not have a deep casserole, then use a suitable mixing bowl and cover it with a plate. The exact amount of water needed does vary with the shape of the dish, so it is worth checking in the second half of the cooking time to make sure the lentils are not becoming too dry. When you have cooked lentils once or twice you will know whether it is necessary to check or not.

The cooking time for smaller or larger quantities is not significantly shorter or longer but you need proportionally more water for smaller quantities and slightly less for large quantities.

Green Lentils Mix 225g/8oz green lentils with 900ml/1½ pints boiling water in a large bowl or casserole dish. Add a little salt, cover (use a plate to cover a mixing bowl) and cook on full for 35–40 minutes. Stir halfway through cooking and check to make sure that the liquid does not dry up before the end of the cooking time. If necessary top up with a little extra boiling water. When cooked the lentils should be moist but all the water should have been absorbed. Toss a knob of butter, plenty of black pepper and some chopped parsley into the lentils.

Lentils with Leeks Wash and slice 225g/8oz leeks and mix with the lentils at the beginning of the cooking time. Add a bay leaf, cook as above and serve topped with soured cream.

Red Lentils Place 225g/8oz red lentils in a large dish with 600ml/1 pint boiling water. Add a little seasoning and cook on full for 15–20 minutes. Stir halfway through cooking and check to make sure that there is enough water towards the end of the cooking time. Beat a knob of butter and plenty of pepper into the lentils before serving.

Spiced Lentils Cook red lentils as above, add 1 finely chopped onion and 2 teaspoons cumin seeds. When the lentils are cooked, place 1 halved and very thinly sliced onion in a basin with 50g/2oz butter or ghee. Add ½ teaspoon cumin seeds and 2 teaspoons ground coriander, then cook on full for 4–5 minutes, stirring once. Pour the onion and spices over the lentils and serve. Mix the lentils with the onion just before they are eaten.

Lentil Pâté Cook the red lentils as above, then beat in 50g/2oz butter, 100g/4oz full fat cream cheese, seasoning to taste, 2 tablespoons snipped chives and a dash of lemon juice. Turn into a dish and leave to cool, then chill thoroughly before serving.

LIVER

Tender lamb's liver cooks well in the microwave but ox liver is best prepared conventionally, in slow-cooked casseroles. Trim and slice the lamb's liver, then turn and rearrange it at least once during cooking; care must be taken not to overcook it.

Defrosting Lamb's Liver Allow 7–9 minutes per 450g/1lb on defrost power. Unwrap the liver and put it in a covered dish. Separate the slices as soon as possible during defrosting and rearrange if necessary. Leave to stand for 5 minutes before cooking.

Cooking Lamb's Liver Trim and slice the liver, then arrange the slices in a dish and dot with butter. Season with pepper, cover and cook on full.

225g/8oz – 2–3 minutes	
450g/1lb – 4–6 minutes	

Liver and Bacon Cook 1 chopped onion and 175g/6oz roughly chopped bacon with 1 tablespoon oil on full for 5 minutes. Stir in 1 tablespoon flour, a dash of Worcestershire sauce, 2 teaspoons tomato purée and 300ml/½ pint boiling stock. Add a little dried sage if you like, then lay 450g/1lb sliced lamb's liver in the dish and spoon the sauce over it. Cover and cook on full for 7–9 minutes, stirring twice.

LOBSTER

A 1.25kg/2½lb lobster is the largest which can be cooked successfully in the microwave. A lobster up to this size can be fitted into a large mixing bowl for cooking. The most humane way of killing a live lobster, other than by dropping it into boiling water, is to put it in the freezer. Put the lobster in a bag in the freezer and leave it there for several hours or overnight until it is frozen hard to ensure that it is dead.

To cook the lobster, place it in a mixing bowl and cook on defrost for 12–14 minutes, depending on size, until the tail is defrosted. Small areas of the lobster will still be icy. Pour 150ml/¼ pint boiling water into the bottom of the bowl, then cover and cook on full until the dark colour of the shell changes to pink. This will take about 7–10 minutes, depending on the size of the lobster. Turn it once during cooking. Allow to cool before splitting and extracting the meat.

Defrosting Cooked Lobster If you buy a frozen lobster in water, then make a small slit in the bag and lay the lobster in a large dish. Cook on defrost for 12–14 minutes, then leave to stand for 5 minutes before using.

Reheating Cooked Lobster Meat Cooked lobster meat can be reheated in sauces in the microwave and the timing is very short – about 1–3 minutes on full depending on the quantities.

M

MACARONI
See Pasta, page 113.

Macaroni Cheese Cook 225g/8oz macaroni following the instructions on page 113. Make a cheese sauce (see page 20) and stir the drained cooked pasta into it. Add 3 tablespoons finely snipped chives or 2 chopped spring onions. Turn into a gratin dish and top with some breadcrumbs and a little grated cheese, then brown under the grill before serving.

> *This is of course an ideal dish to make in advance and then reheat in the microwave. Allow 2–3 minutes on full, longer if reheating from frozen.*

MACKEREL

Like other fish this cooks very well in the micro-wave, either whole or filleted. For best results roll mackerel fillets. The whole fish can be cooked with or without their heads; the advantage of having the heads cut off is that the fish are smaller and fit better into a suitable dish. Make two or three slashes into the skin of whole fish before cooking. Season the inside of whole mackerel or the fillets before rolling with pepper, chopped fresh parsley, rosemary or dill and a dash of lemon juice. Sprinkle with 2 tablespoons water, secure rolls with wooden cocktail sticks, and cover the dish. Cook on full for the following times:

Whole Fish	1	2–4 minutes
	2	4–6 minutes
	3	5–7 minutes
	4	7–9 minutes
Rolled Fillets (2 from each fish)	2	2–3 minutes
	4	3–5 minutes
	6	5–6 minutes
	8	6–8 minutes

Note Arrange fish rolls as far apart as possible round the outer edge of the dish.

MANGETOUT PEAS

Trim and wash the mangetout, then place in a dish with 2 tablespoons water and cover. Cook on full power.

100g/4oz – 2–3 minutes
225g/8oz – 4–6 minutes

The cooked mangetout should be crisp not soft.

MANGO
See Chutney, page 46.

MARMALADE
Although you will find recipes for making marmalade in the microwave, it is more trouble than it is worth to try and successfully boil large quantities of preserves in this way. So stick to traditional methods for boiling until set. However, you may find the microwave useful for softening the fruit rind. The timing depends on the quantity and the cut – finely shredded rind cooks best. Place the rind in a bowl with enough boiling water to cover it generously, taken from the measured quantity suggested in the recipe. Add all the fruit trimmings (pulp, pith and pips) tied in muslin, cover the bowl and allow about 15–20 minutes on full. Make sure there is plenty of water in the bowl all the time. Leave to cool, then squeeze all juice from the bag of trimmings and continue to cook the marmalade conventionally.

MARROW
Cubed marrow or marrow rings can be cooked with great success in the microwave. It is also possible to cook a small whole marrow but do check that it will fit into the microwave before you prepare a stuffing for it!

Marrow Cubes Place the prepared vegetable in a dish, add 2 tablespoons water and cover the dish. Cook on full.

225g/8oz – 3–5 minutes	
450g/1lb – 7–10 minutes	

Drain the cooked marrow and toss with butter and seasoning. Good topped with cheese sauce and grilled to brown.

Stuffed Marrow Rings Cut slices about 3.5cm/1½in

thick. Peel and scoop out the seeds. Arrange as far apart as possible in a dish and dot with butter. Cover and cook on full.

1 ring – 3–5 minutes	
2 rings – 5–7 minutes	
3 rings – 6–8 minutes	
4 rings – 7–10 minutes	

After cooking, fill the middle with a stuffing of cooked ingredients (for example rice with herbs, vegetables and chopped ham; a breadcrumb and herb stuffing; cooked lentils with herbs and moz-zarella cheese), baste with butter and re-cover the dish. Heat on full for 1–3 minutes, or until the filling is hot, before serving.

MARZIPAN

Soften slightly stale, hardened marzipan (or almond paste) by heating for a few seconds in the microwave. Remember to remove all foil wrapping and place the block of paste on a plate. Using full power allow 5–10 seconds at first, then repeat as necessary.

'MEAT

See Beef page 20; Lamb, page 94; and Pork, page 120.

Tender cuts of meat can be cooked successfully in the microwave but the result is not browned and the flavour is similar to that which would be achieved by steaming. Whether or not you like microwave cooked meat depends to a large extent on personal preference.

Small cuts – chops, steaks etc – which are to be eaten plain, without any sauce or flavouring, are probably best cooked conventionally for crisp browned results. Cooked with a sauce, however, these cuts do very well in the microwave. A browning dish is useful if you do want to cook these cuts without additional ingredients.

Joints can be cooked in the microwave to give reasonably tender results and with very slight browning if the piece of meat is large enough for the outside of the fat to begin to 'fry' itself. For best results use the microwave to part-cook the meat, then finish it in a conventional oven.

Mince cooks very well in the microwave, either beef, pork or lamb; as burgers, meatballs or a sauce.

Stewing cuts cannot be cooked with great success. Tough cuts which require lengthy cooking should be avoided. Braising cuts can be cooked on a medium or low setting for up to 1 hour but the result is inferior to that expected of conventional cooking.

> *Do not season meat with salt before cooking, unless you are adding the salt to a significant quantity of sauce (for example when cooking chops in a casserole).*

MELBA SAUCE

Good with ice cream or steamed sponge pudding. Place 450g/1lb raspberries in a bowl with 50g/2oz icing sugar. Cover and cook on full for 5 minutes. Cool slightly before pressing through a sieve. Taste and add extra sugar if necessary. Cool and chill before serving.

METAL

Do not use metal in the microwave. Avoid all dishes or packaging which has metal trimmings or decoration. The only exceptions to this rule are when using small pieces of cooking foil to shield small areas of food, or when following the microwave manufacturer's instructions on the use of shallow foil containers for heating convenience foods.

MILK
Pour the milk into a suitable jug and heat on full. Stand near to ensure that the milk does not boil over.

150ml/¼ pint – about 1 minute	
300ml/½ pint – 2–3 minutes	
600ml/1 pint – 4–6 minutes	

MINCE
This cooks very well in the microwave. Follow instructions for Minced Beef (page 22) for all types of mince.

MULLET
Whole grey mullet are moist white fish which will serve between two and four people depending on their size. A fish which fits into the microwave will usually provide two portions. Cook two fish separately if necessary – the time is short and the first will not have cooled if transferred to a heated serving plate and covered, before the second fish is ready. Small red mullet also cook well in the microwave and four of these can be cooked in one dish.

Scrape the scales off the fish, rinse and pat dry. Place a bay leaf or two in the body cavity and sprinkle with a squeeze of lemon. Slash both sides of the skin two or three times. Place in a dish, dot with butter and top with slices of lemon and sprigs of parsley for flavour. Cover and cook on full. Pierce the flesh at the thickest part to see if it is cooked – it should flake easily but still be very slightly undercooked. The few minutes taken to serve the fish will allow the residual heat to complete the cooking.

1 grey mullet	9–11 minutes
(about 1–1.5kg/2–3lb)	

2 medium red mullet	8–10 minutes
4 medium red mullet	12–15 minutes

Note If the red mullet are very small reduce the above times by 1–2 minutes in each case.

MUSHROOMS

Whole or sliced, mushrooms cook quickly in the microwave.

Whole Button Mushrooms Mix with olive oil or butter and crushed garlic. Add freshly ground black pepper and toss with chopped parsley after cooking. Cook on full and serve hot or cold.

225g/8oz – 2–4 minutes
450g/1lb – 4–6 minutes

Sliced Mushrooms Heat 25–50g/1–2oz butter on full for 30–60 seconds. Add the mushrooms and cook on full.

100g/4oz – 1–2 minutes
225g/8oz – 2–4 minutes
350g/12oz – 3–5 minutes
450g/1lb   – 4–6 minutes

Stuffed Mushrooms Wipe open mushrooms and arrange as far apart as possible in a buttered dish. Fill with fresh breadcrumbs mixed with a little melted butter, crushed garlic, chopped fresh herbs and a few chopped walnuts if you like. Cook on full. Garnish with tomato.

2 mushrooms – 1–2 minutes
4 mushrooms – 2–4 minutes
6 mushrooms – 4–6 minutes

MUSSELS

These cook with success in the microwave. They should be scrubbed, beards removed and any which are open and do not shut when tapped must be discarded. Place in a large bowl with 150ml/¼ pint hot liquid. Cover and cook on full, allowing 3–5 minutes for 1 kg/2lb. Shake the bowl twice during cooking to rearrange the mussels. When ready the shellfish should have opened; discard any which are not opened.

Moules à la Marinière Use dry white wine, add a bay leaf, ½ finely chopped onion, 2 chopped cloves garlic and 1 small finely chopped carrot. Heat for 2 minutes on full before adding the scrubbed mussels and cooking as above. Sprinkle with parsley before serving.

OKRA

These green pod-shaped vegetables are also known as lady's fingers. Only small, young okra should be selected for the best results as they can be quite tough when large, very dark green and old. Avoid bruised vegetables. They are sliced and added to casseroles and the natural gum-like substance which they contain acts as a thickening. If they are to be served plain, they are best cooked whole, otherwise they can be slimy.

Trim off the stalk end without cutting the end off the pod. Finely chop 1 onion and cook it on full with 25g/1oz butter for 3 minutes. Add 450g/1lb okra, 2 tablespoons lemon juice and some freshly ground black pepper. Mix well, cover the dish and cook on full for 3–5 minutes, stirring halfway through. The okra should be tender but still firm. Add a little salt before serving. Good with spiced dishes and rice.

OMELETTES

It is not recommended to cook an omelette in the microwave. It is possible to pour egg into a shallow dish and cook it until set, but the result cannot be compared to an omelette which is cooked in a very hot, lightly greased pan on the hob.

ONIONS

When onions are used in a dish which is cooked in the microwave the rule is to cook them first. By doing this the flavour of raw onion will not dominate the rest of the food. Chopped onions give slightly better results than slices. Place a chopped onion in a dish with 1–2 tablespoons oil or 25g/1oz butter or margarine. Mix lightly, then cook on full for 3 minutes. For those who are following a diet which excludes fat, add 1 tablespoon water to the onion and cover the dish.

Whole Onions These cook very well and they are delicious served very simply topped with butter and plenty of freshly ground black pepper. Peel the onions and place them in a dish with 2 tablespoons water. Cover and cook on full.

1 –	2–3 minutes
2 –	4–5 minutes
3 –	5–6 minutes
4 –	7–9 minutes

The middles of the cooked onions can be scooped out, chopped and combined with breadcrumbs, walnuts, parsley and a little Parmesan cheese to make a delicious stuffing. The stuffed onions should be heated for 1–2 minutes on full, until the stuffing is hot.

Glazed Onions Small whole pickling onions make a good vegetable dish. Place 450g/1lb peeled onions in a dish with 50g/2oz butter, 1 tablespoon water and 2 teaspoons sugar. Cover and cook on full for 10–12 minutes, stirring twice, until all the onions are tender. Halve the ingredients for 225g/8oz onions and cook in the same way, allowing 6–8 minutes.

Onion Sauce See page 20.

ORANGES

Caramelised Oranges Peel and slice 1 orange per person, removing all pith and pips. Either re-shape the oranges and place them in a heatproof dish or lay the slices in the dish. Sprinkle any juice over them. Make a caramel (see page 33), pour it over the oranges and allow to cool slightly. Cover and cool completely, then chill the fruit overnight by which time the caramel will have softened. Sprinkle with shredded orange rind or flaked almonds before serving with whipped cream or yogurt.

OXTAIL

Oxtail is a tough cut and needs long, slow cooking by traditional methods.

PAELLA

This can be made with great success in the microwave. If you want to use fresh mussels, then cook them first following the directions on page 109. Cook 1 chopped onion, 1 diced green pepper and 1 crushed clove garlic with 3 tablespoons olive oil on full for 5 minutes. Add 225g/8oz long-grain rice and 2 boneless chicken breasts. Mix ¼ teaspoon powdered saffron with 450ml/¾ pint boiling chicken stock and pour it over the rice. Cover and cook on full for 10 minutes. Dice the chicken, then lightly mix it with the rice and add 225g/8oz peeled cooked prawns, 225g/8oz cooked mussels and 175g/6oz frozen peas. Cover and cook on full for a further 7–10 minutes, until the liquid is absorbed and all the ingredients are cooked. Adjust the seasoning and serve.

PANCAKES
Pancakes cannot be cooked in the microwave. Sauce-based savoury fillings, stewed apples or other fruit can be cooked in the microwave to fill pancakes that are made conventionally. Heat the filled pancakes for 1–2 minutes on full before serving.

Frozen pancakes can be defrosted in the microwave for a few seconds on full, so they are just soft enough to fold around a filling. If they are to be eaten plain the pancakes are best heated by placing them still frozen in a frying pan with a little hot butter and cooking over the hob.

PARSNIPS
Trim and peel the parsnips, then slice them or cut into chunks. Place in a dish with 3 tablespoons water and cook, covered, on full.

450g/1lb	– 7–10 minutes
675g/1½lb	– 12–15 minutes

Leave to stand, still covered, for 3 minutes, then drain and mash the parsnips or toss them in butter.

PASTA

Large amounts of pasta, either dried or fresh, are best cooked by conventional methods. Similarly, long spaghetti and sheets of lasagne benefit from being swirled into a very large saucepan of boiling water. Small shapes, cannelloni, broken macaroni and nests of noodles can be cooked in the microwave in a large casserole or mixing bowl. The pasta should be well covered with plenty of freshly boiled water and a little salt can be added. The cooking time is not significantly less, as the pasta needs time to absorb water and soften; the advantage is that, in a large enough bowl, the pasta is not likely to boil over. For 100–225g/4–8oz allow the following times on full, then leave the pasta to stand in its cooking liquid for 5 minutes before straining and serving.

Dried noodles (tagliatelle)	5–7 minutes
Dried short-cut macaroni and shapes	10–12 minutes
Cannelloni tubes (4–8)	8–10 minutes
Chinese egg noodles in a block (thin, oriental-style egg noodles are ready when they separate into curly strands and they should stand for 2–3 minutes before draining)	2 minutes
Fresh pasta noodles	3–5 minutes
Fresh pasta shapes	4–6 minutes
Stuffed fresh pasta (fresh pasta should stand for 2–3 minutes, then check that it is just tender before draining)	5–7 minutes

PASTRY

See Combination Microwave Cooking, page 50.

Shortcrust, flaky, puff and choux pastries cannot be cooked in the microwave. Choux will not retain its rise and shape. Puff and flaky will retain their rise until overcooked and dried out. Shortcrust pastry does not follow this pattern of disasters but it does not have the same flavour or texture as pastry cooked conventionally. By the time it becomes crisp and crumbly in texture it has, in fact, thoroughly overcooked and dried out. The cooked pastry tastes of raw flour and it is not browned.

Defrosting Puff or Shortcrust Pastry Unwrap the pastry and place it on a double-thick piece of absorbent kitchen paper. Microwave on defrost setting and turn the pastry over once or twice during defrosting.

225g/8oz – 2–4 minutes	
450g/1lb – 5–6 minutes	

PÂTÉS
See Chicken Liver Pâté, page 44.

Small pâtés can be cooked in the microwave but the ingredients should be part-cooked before they are minced and combined. This way a good result is achieved with a very short cooking time.

Brandied Pâté Combine 675g/1½lb diced pork with 225g/8oz trimmed and diced pig's liver. Add 1 finely chopped onion, a bay leaf, 2 crushed cloves garlic and 25g/1oz butter. Cover and cook on full for 17–20 minutes, stirring twice, until the meat is just cooked. Mince the meats and onion, then mix with 3 tablespoons brandy, 50g/2oz fresh breadcrumbs, seasoning, ½ teaspoon ground mace, and a beaten egg. Press the pâté into a dish. Cover and cook on full for 3–6 minutes, until the pâté is firm. Weight the pâté, leave it to cool, then chill overnight. Serve with Melba Toast.

PEACHES
Poached Peaches Heat 150 ml/¼ pint water or wine with 75g/3oz sugar and a strip of lemon rind for 2–3 minutes on full, until the sugar has dissolved. Stir well, add 4 peeled, stoned and halved peaches and cover the dish. Cook on full for 3–5 minutes, until the fruit is hot and tender. The cooking time depends on the ripeness of the fruit. For 2 peaches allow about 2 minutes cooking.

Stuffed Peaches Peel and halve 2 peaches, then brush them with lemon juice. Place in a dish, cut sides uppermost (cut a fine sliver off the rounded side of each half if they will not sit evenly) and fill with crushed macaroons moistened with a little sherry, rum or ginger wine. Cover and cook on full for about 2 minutes, until the fruit is hot. Serve with cream, chocolate sauce (see page 46) or Melba sauce (see page 106).

PEANUT CRUNCH
Mix 225g/8oz sugar with 8 tablespoons water in a dish. Make sure that the dish will withstand the heat of the caramel. Cook on full for 3–5 minutes, stir well, then cook for a further 10–15 minutes, until the syrup forms a caramel. Watch the mixture closely to prevent it from burning. Add 25g/1oz butter and 100g/4oz roughly chopped salted peanuts. Stir in ¼ teaspoon bicarbonate of soda and pour the mixture into a greased tin. Leave until cool, then break up and store in an airtight container.

PEARS
Pears can be poached very successfully in the microwave. Cook 100g/4oz sugar with 150ml/¼ pint liquid for 1–2 minutes, until the sugar dissolves. Use red wine, cider, water or orange juice to make the syrup. Add peeled, cored, whole firm pears

(leave their stalks on), cover the dish and cook on full, rearranging the fruit once.

2 pears – 3–5 minutes	
4 pears – 7–10 minutes	

The syrup is good flavoured with orange rind, cinnamon sticks and cloves.

PEAS

Fresh and frozen peas cook well in the microwave and canned peas can be heated rapidly. Place the peas in a dish, adding 3 tablespoons water to fresh vegetables. Frozen peas do not require liquid and canned peas should be heated in the liquid from the can, but transferred to a dish. Cover and cook on full, stirring halfway through the time.

Fresh peas

225g/8oz	– 4–6 minutes
450g/1lb	– 7–10 minutes

Frozen peas

50g/2oz	– 2–3 minutes
100g/4oz	– 3–4 minutes
225g/8oz	– 4–6 minutes
350g/12oz	– 5–7 minutes
450g/1lb	– 7–10 minutes

Canned peas

Small can – about 2 minutes	
Large can – about 3–4 minutes	

Drain the peas and toss them with butter before serving. If you like add a sprig of mint to the dish while the vegetables are cooking.

PEPPERS

When they are part of a cooked dish peppers should be treated in the same way as onions for best results; cook the diced or sliced peppers with a little oil or butter before adding the remaining ingredients. Since recipes which call for peppers usually include onions then it is best to cook both together, allowing 5 minutes on full for 1 pepper combined with 1 onion.

Stuffed Pepper Halves These make a good side dish or first course – I prefer them to whole stuffed peppers as there can be plenty of stuffing to each pepper half, giving a better balance of flavour. Halve two large peppers lengthways and remove all seeds and pith, leaving the stalks in place. Place in a dish, add 2 tablespoons water and cover. Cook on full for 4–6 minutes, until just tender. Do not cook the peppers until they are very soft or they will not retain their shape. Leave them to stand in the closely covered dish for 5 minutes. The stuffing can be varied to suit your taste but it should consist of cooked ingredients. Flaked tuna and sliced mushrooms in cheese sauce makes a delicious filling (allow 300ml/½ pint sauce, serving any extra separately) – add 50g/2oz fresh breadcrumbs and a squeeze of lemon juice before filling the shells. The peppers should be drained before filling, then heated for 1–2 minutes before serving.

Alternatively, mix freshly cooked rice with diced cooked ham, chopped peeled tomatoes and chopped spring onion, then spoon this stuffing into the pepper halves. Top each with a slice of mozzarella cheese and brown under a hot grill before serving.

Meat-stuffed Peppers Cut the tops off 4 peppers and scoop out the seeds and pith from inside. Stand the shells in a large, deep dish. Cook 1 chopped onion, 1 crushed clove garlic and 2 tablespoons oil for 3 minutes on full. Stir in 350g/12oz minced beef, cover and cook on full for 4–6 minutes, until the mince is part-cooked. Stir in 100g/4oz chopped mushrooms, 4 peeled and chopped tomatoes, seasoning, 50g/2oz grated cheese and 50g/2oz fresh breadcrumbs. Divide this stuffing between the peppers, spoon 2 tablespoons around the vegetables and cover the dish. The sliced off pepper caps can be replaced on top of the stuffing if you like (alternatively they can be chopped and mixed with the meat). Cook on full for 9–11 minutes, until the peppers and the filling are cooked through.

1 pepper (quarter the stuffing)– 2–4 minutes
2 peppers (halve the stuffing) – 5–7 minutes

PETITS POIS
See Peas, page 116.

PICCALILLI
This is one traditional preserve which cooks very well in the microwave. Break 225g/8oz cauliflower into small florets, dice ½ small cucumber and 1 large carrot, and chop 1 onion. Place the vegetables in a bowl and sprinkle with salt. Leave overnight, then drain, rinse and dry thoroughly. Mix 1 tablespoon flour with ¼ teaspoon turmeric, ¼ teaspoon ground ginger and 1 teaspoon mustard powder. Gradually stir in 150ml/¼ pint cider vinegar, making a smooth paste. Add 100g/4oz sugar and stir well. Cook on full for 3–5 minutes, whisking once until the sauce is boiling and thickened and the sugar has dissolved. Add the vegetables, mix well and cover the dish. Cook on full for 5–8 minutes, stirring halfway through cooking. The vegetables should be just tender but still crunchy. Pot at once and cover immediately with airtight lids. The preserve should be stored for

at least a week before it is eaten and it will keep for up to 3 months in a cool, dry place (unopened).

PITTA BREAD

Warm pitta bread in the microwave: lay the breads flat on absorbent kitchen paper and cover with a second piece of paper. Cook on full.

1 piece – 15–20 seconds	
2 pieces – 30–60 seconds	
3 pieces – 1–1½ minutes	
4 pieces – 1½–2 minutes	

PLAICE

Plaice fillets cook very well in the microwave. Arrange the fillets in a dish, folding the thin tails right under to prevent them overcooking. Dot with butter, sprinkle with pepper and a little lemon juice (but do not add salt) and add bay leaves, tarragon or parsley sprigs for flavour. Cover the dish and cook the fish on full.

2 fillets – 1–2 minutes	
4 fillets – 3–5 minutes	
6 fillets – 4–6 minutes	
8 fillets – 7–9 minutes	

When cooking 6 fillets or more, for even results roll the fillets and secure with wooden cocktail sticks. Turn and rearrange the fish halfway through cooking – the exact time will depend on the size and thickness of the fillets but the above guide is for plump fillets. When cooked the fish should flake easily but still be slightly opaque towards the base of the flakes.

Defrosting Plaice See page 75, following instructions for defrosting fish fillets.

PLUMS

Poach plums in syrup in the microwave. Heat
75g/3oz sugar with 100ml/4fl oz water on full for
about 2 minutes, until the sugar has dissolved. Add
halved and stoned plums, cover the dish and cook
on full, stirring halfway through cooking.

225g/8oz – 2–4 minutes	
450g/1lb – 4–6 minutes	

The fruit can be cooked whole but the skins should
be split to prevent them bursting.

Frozen Plums These fall easily once defrosted so they
will not hold their shape well enough to be served as
a fruit compote, but they can be puréed and turned
into a delicious fool by mixing with custard or
cream. Do not cook in syrup, but place the fruit in a
covered dish and sweeten after cooking. Follow the
timings given above.

POPADUMS

Popadums can be puffed very successfully in the
microwave. Cook the smaller popadums in pairs or
the large ones individually. Place the popadum on a
piece of absorbent kitchen paper and cook on full
for 30 seconds, turn it over and cook for a further
20–30 seconds, or until evenly puffed. The popadum
will feel slightly soft when first removed from the
microwave but it crisps up in a few seconds.

PORK

Most cuts of pork are tender enough for microwave
cooking but they must be trimmed of excess fat and
all gristle before cooking. Sinews and membranes
should also be removed from the meat.

Defrosting Pork The meat should be unwrapped and

placed in a dish, then covered. Turn joints once or twice during defrosting and shield any thin areas if they start to get hot. Separate chops or small cuts as soon as possible and spread out. Use defrost setting then leave the meat to stand for 20–30 minutes before cooking. It should be very cold and just slightly icy when ready.

Joints	per 450g/1lb	6–8 minutes
Chops or small cuts	per 450g/1lb	7–9 minutes

Cooking Pork As with other large joints of meat, best results are obtained by half cooking the pork in the microwave, then finishing it off in the conventional oven. Small cuts are best if they are cooked in a sauce in which case the lack of browning is not too obvious. A browning dish can be used, following the manufacturer's instructions, or chops can be browned quickly by rolling on the surface of a hot frying pan on the hob before being casseroled in the microwave. The following times are a guide to cooking on full:

Joints	per 450g/1lb	7–10 minutes
Small cuts	per 450g/1lb	6–8 minutes

Allow small cuts to stand for 5–10 minutes before serving and leave joints for 25–30 minutes. Check to make sure that the meat is cooked through by piercing the centre of the joint after the standing time. If there is any sign of blood, then cook the meat for a few minutes and check it again.

Minced Pork See Beef, page 20, and follow instructions for mince.

PORRIDGE

Porridge cooks very well in the microwave but it is important to allow plenty of room for it to boil, particularly when using milk and making a large amount. A single portion can be cooked in a large cereal bowl or in a basin.

For a generous portion place 50g/2oz porridge oats in a basin and stir in 300ml/½ pint milk or water, or half and half. Add ½ teaspoon salt and cook on full for 2½–4½ minutes, stirring once. Stir well at the end of cooking by which time the oats should be cooked and the porridge thickened.

Double the quantities for 2–3 servings and allow 4–6 minutes on full. Three times the above quantities will serve 4 and allow 7–10 minutes cooking time.

POTATOES

Cook jacket potatoes in the microwave, then crisp their skin under a hot grill if you like. Diced or sliced potatoes cook very successfully and small new potatoes can be cooked to perfection. For a large amount of mashed potato it is best to boil the potatoes conventionally, so that they become very soft and mash easily without any lumps.

> *When the conventional oven is hot, roast a large batch of potatoes, allow to cool and freeze them. Defrost and reheat in the microwave, then pop them under a hot grill for a minute or two before serving if you like.*

Jacket Potatoes Scrub and prick large potatoes (about 350g/12oz each) and place them on absorbent kitchen paper on the turntable or floor of the microwave. Spread the potatoes as far apart as possible if cooking more than one, and turn them over halfway through cooking. Cook on full power for the following times:

1 potato – 6–8 minutes

2 potatoes – 10–12 minutes
3 potatoes – 14–16 minutes
4 potatoes – 20–22 minutes

Old Potatoes Cut into large chunks, dice or slice – it is important to make sure the pieces of potato are fairly even in size. Place in a dish and add 3 tablespoons water. Do not add salt. Cover and cook on full, rearranging the potatoes once or twice during cooking.

450g/1lb – 6–8 minutes
675g/1½lb – 7–10 minutes
1kg/2lb – 12–14 minutes

New Potatoes Scrub evenly sized new potatoes and place in a dish with 3 tablespoons water. Do not add salt. Cover and cook on full, rearranging once or twice.

450g/1lb – 5–7 minutes
675g/1½lb – 6–9 minutes
1kg/2lb – 8–11 minutes

Small new potatoes take slightly less time than evenly cut old potatoes.

Instant Mash Look out for the manufacturer's instructions for microwave cooking, as many brands are specifically tested by this method and advice is given for the product.

To make up a 90g/3½oz packet, place the dried potato in a large basin and stir in 450ml/¾ pint cold water. Cook on full for 6–8 minutes, stirring frequently, until the potato is thick and hot.

Frozen Roast Potatoes The potatoes should be cooked until nicely crisp before they are frozen. Place on a double thickness of absorbent kitchen paper in a dish and cover with absorbent kitchen paper. Cook on full.

225g/8oz – 3–5 minutes	
450g/1lb – 7–9 minutes	

Remove all the paper and crisp the tops of the potatoes under a hot grill if you like.

POWER SETTINGS

Each manufacturer uses their own set of terms for expressing the different cooking settings on microwave cookers. Read the instruction book carefully to determine which are the most and least powerful settings and which setting is recommended for defrosting.

In this book the terms full, medium-high, medium and defrost are used. Full power is 100%, medium power is 50% of the total available and defrost is 30%. Medium-high is about 70% of the total. Most microwaves have a power setting below defrost, at 20–25%, and this is intended to keep food warm once it has cooked but before it is to be served.

Cooking times given are for 650–700 watt ovens. Always start by cooking the food for the shortest suggested time, then continue to cook it if necessary. Remember you cannot ruin food by removing it from the microwave before it is fully cooked but you can end up with a disaster if you overcook something.

The time taken to cook food is affected by various factors. Individual ovens do vary in results, even if they give the same power output. The cooking container can change the time – its shape will affect the way in which the food is distributed and whether it cooks evenly or not; certain containers specifically designed for use in the microwave are made from materials which allow the microwaves to pass through most efficiently and this can slightly shorten the cooking time.

The size of the oven cavity affects the cooking time. If you have a low-powered oven (for example 500 watt), then you will have to increase the cooking times given but do compare them with the times in the manufacturer's handbook. A small microwave with a low power output can sometimes cook almost as quickly as a larger one with a greater power output. As a general guide, some 600 watt ovens cook almost as quickly as 650 watt ovens, so you will have to increase the times given very slightly if you have a 600 watt oven. There is a significant difference between cooking times in 600 and 700 watt ovens. Ovens rated above 700 watts are particularly speedy and you should shorten the times given. It is as well to make a note of certain timings which you use frequently and which apply specifically to your oven.

PRALINE

Follow the instructions for Peanut Crunch, see page 115, substituting split, blanched almonds for the peanuts. Omit the butter and bicarbonate of soda, then pour the praline on to a tin, in a thin layer, and leave until cold. Crush or break the hard praline with a rolling pin or toffee hammer.

PRAWNS

Peeled cooked prawns toughen if they are over-heated. They can be added to a savoury sauce along with other cooked fish or seafood and served with rice or pasta, or used as a pie filling. Heated briefly in garlic and lemon butter they make a delicious first course, either served simply with crusty bread or used as a filling for halved avocados.

Defrosting Prawns Prawns are usually best used straight from frozen if they are to be thoroughly reheated in a dish. However, for cocktails and cold recipes defrost them first; spread out on a shallow dish, cover with absorbent kitchen paper and use defrost setting.

225g/8oz – 4–6 minutes	
450g/1lb – 7–9 minutes	

> *To defrost a small quantity of prawns rapidly, place them in a basin and use full power, allowing 1–2 minutes for 225g/8oz. Drain the prawns and gently rub any bits of ice off them, then pat dry on absorbent kitchen paper.*

PRESERVES
See Chutney, page 46; Jam, page 90; and Piccalilli, page 118.

The microwave can be used to prepare small quantities of some preserves but it is not recommended for preserving large quantities of produce in the trāditional sense.

PRESSURE COOKER
A pressure cooker designed specifically for use in the microwave oven is available (also known as a tender cooker). It works on the same principle as the traditional pressure cooker but using a lower pressure to cook food. Until I tested it I thought the pressure cooker was just another average accessory of questionable value. Then I cooked a stew – 450g/1lb shin of beef, cut into small cubes, 225g/8oz lamb's kidneys, 1 chopped onion (cooked first for 3 minutes on full with a drop of oil), 2 tablespoons flour, salt and pepper, a bay leaf, some parsley and 600ml/1 pint boiling stock. Following the manufacturer's instructions closely, I cooked my stew on full for 30 minutes and the result was excellent. The

meat was thoroughly tenderised – as good as if I had cooked it conventionally – it had given up its flavour to the liquid and the flavour of the stew was excellent. I also cooked braising steak, again cut into small cubes, in the same way and that cooked well in 20 minutes and was melt-in-the-mouth tender after 25 minutes.

The pressure cooker overcomes one of the great disadvantages of cooking meat in the microwave. It prevents the microwaves from toughening the meat and it actually tenderises the food thoroughly. I tested it on the least glamorous recipe – I did not bother to brown the meat first, I just threw all the ingredients into the cooker (apart from the onion as the taste of raw onion dominates any dish). The time saving compared to traditional methods is enormous, making this a particularly economical way of cooking a stew or other cuts which traditionally take hours. Care has to be taken not to overfill the cooker and to avoid too much food which will froth up and block the vent. The pressure cooker is not at the cheap end of the cooking dishes range but it is not ridiculously expensive, and the results and potential for saving on fuel make it the best accessory that I have yet discovered for the microwave.

As well as stewing beef, the pressure cooker can be used to cook other meats, poultry, vegetables, rice, soups and desserts. It is designed to hold up to 1.5kg/3lb meat and it is dishwasher safe. I am now going to experiment further!

PRUNES

Dried prunes can be cooked in the microwave without pre-soaking. Place 225g/8oz prunes in a large dish and cover with plenty of water (about 450ml/¾ pint, depending on the shape of the cooking container). Cover and cook on full for 15–20 minutes, then leave to stand for 10 minutes.

PULSES
See Beans, dried, page 17.

PUMPKIN
Cubed pumpkin flesh cooks well in the microwave. All peel and pips should be removed and the pumpkin cut into evenly sized cubes. Place in a covered dish and cook on full, allowing 7–9 minutes for 450g/1lb.

The pumpkin can be served as a vegetable, tossed in butter and pepper, or used as required. Alternatively, cook a chopped onion in 25g/1oz butter for 3 minutes on full before adding and cooking the pumpkin. Sprinkle with a little grated cheese and some fresh breadcrumbs, then brown the top under a hot grill.

PUNCH
Punch can be heated in a mixing bowl in the microwave or individual glasses can be warmed for 30 seconds.

> *Remember not to use cut glass or very delicate glassware in the microwave.*

Cider Punch Cut a dessert apple into quarters and stud each piece with 2 cloves. Place in a bowl and add a cinnamon stick and the pared rind from 1 orange. Add the juice of the orange, 25–50g/1–2oz sugar (to taste) and a bottle (1 litre/35.2fl oz) of medium-sweet cider. Heat on full for 6–8 minutes, stirring once. Leave to stand for 5 minutes before serving. The punch can be reheated for 1 minute on full as it cools.

Mulled Wine Stick an orange with 8 cloves and

place it in a bowl with a cinnamon stick, sugar to taste and a good dash of rum or brandy. Pour in a bottle of red wine and stir well. Heat on full for 5–7 minutes, stirring once. Leave to stand for 5 minutes before serving. This mulled wine is particularly good if made about an hour before needed, then warmed through again just before it is served.

QUICHE
See Flans, Savoury, page 77.

RABBIT
Rabbit meat is tender and therefore cooks well in the microwave, but for best results it should be cooked in a sauce. Boneless, cubed rabbit is ideal or neat rabbit portions can be used.

Rabbit Casserole Cook 1 chopped onion with 100g/4oz diced bacon on full for 5 minutes. Stir in 2 tablespoons flour and 300ml/½ pint boiling stock. Add 450g/1lb cubed boneless rabbit, 1 bay leaf, salt and pepper and 2 tablespoons wholegrain or Dijon mustard. Cover and cook on full for 10–12 minutes, stirring halfway through. The rabbit should be about three-quarters cooked at this stage. Add 100g/4oz frozen peas and re-cover the dish, then cook for a further 4–6 minutes on full, until the rabbit and peas are cooked. Good with pasta, rice or jacket potatoes.

RAISINS
Plump up raisins before adding them to cakes. Put the dried fruit in a basin and sprinkle with a little water. Cover and cook on full for about 1 minute, depending on quantity, until the raisins are soft, warm and plump.

RASPBERRIES
See Melba Sauce, page 106.

These require the minimum of cooking. Prepare a fruit syrup from 75–100g/3–4oz sugar and 150ml/¼ pint water. Cook on full for about 2 minutes, then stir until the sugar has dissolved. Add 450g/1lb raspberries, tossing them gently to coat all the fruit in syrup. Cover and cook on full for 1–3 minutes, stirring once. The time taken to heat the fruit will depend on its ripeness.

Frozen Raspberries These can be poached from frozen as above, allowing 3–5 minutes once the fruit is added to the syrup.

To defrost frozen raspberries, spread them out on a large shallow dish and use defrost setting. Carefully rearrange the fruit halfway through defrosting, then leave it to stand for 10 minutes before using.

225g/8oz – 3–5 minutes	
450g/1lb – 5–7 minutes	

RATATOUILLE
Cut 350g/12oz aubergines into chunks, salt the chunks, leave to stand for 30 minutes, then rinse and dry them. Place 1 chopped onion, 1 bay leaf, 1 diced green pepper, 2 crushed cloves garlic and 6 tablespoons olive oil in a large dish. Cover and cook on

full for 5 minutes. Add the aubergines and 450g/1lb peeled and roughly chopped tomatoes. Cover and cook on full for 10 minutes, stirring once. Add 225g/8oz sliced courgettes, plenty of chopped parsley and black pepper to taste. Cover and cook on full for a further 4–6 minutes, until all the vegetables are cooked. Season to taste with salt and leave to stand for 5 minutes before serving. Chopped mint, fresh marjoram or basil are all delicious in the ratatouille, instead of or as well as the parsley.

RAVIOLI
Turn a 425g/15oz can of ravioli into a dish, cover and heat on full for 3–5 minutes, stirring once. Serve on toast, or top the pasta with grated cheese and brown it under the grill, then serve with French bread.

REDCURRANTS
Follow the cooking instructions for blackcurrants, see page 25.

RED KIDNEY BEANS
Dried red kidney beans can be cooked in the microwave but there is very little advantage in terms of timing and it is essential to make sure that they are well boiled to destroy their natural toxins.

The beans should be soaked for several hours, then placed in a large dish and covered with plenty of fresh boiling water. Cover and cook on full for 10 minutes, watching to ensure that all the beans are boiled for at least 5 minutes. The beans should be cooked on medium-high setting for a further 35–40 minutes, or until they are tender. Make sure that there is plenty of water covering the beans all through cooking and add extra boiling water if necessary.

Canned beans can be reheated with great success in the microwave, usually as part of a meat or vegetable dish.

RHUBARB

Cut the fruit into chunks and place in a dish with sugar, allowing about 100g/4oz per 450g/1lb, or to taste. Cover and cook on full, stirring halfway through cooking.

225g/8oz – 3–5 minutes	
450g/1lb – 6–8 minutes	

Leave the fruit to stand for a few minutes before serving. The exact timing depends on the fruit. Add a little water to tougher, old rhubarb and allow slightly longer cooking time to soften the fruit.

RICE

Rice cooks really well in the microwave. The time saving is not amazing, but the grains do not stick to the cooking dish as they can do to a saucepan and it is easy to cook the rice to perfection. Place the rice in a large dish with cold water. Allow 600ml/1 pint water for each 225g/8oz white long-grain rice and 750ml/1¼ pints for brown rice. Add a little salt to taste and cover the dish. Make sure there is plenty of room for the water to boil up as it cooks without spilling over the edge of the dish. Cook on full.

White rice, basmati rice, risotto rice	100g/4oz	8–10 mins
White rice, basmati rice, risotto rice	225g/8oz	12–15 mins
Brown rice	100g/4oz	16–20 mins
Brown rice	225g/8oz	22–25 mins
Wild rice	100g/4oz	25–30 mins

Wild rice	225g/8oz	35–40 mins

Check the rice halfway through cooking to make sure there is enough liquid, then leave it to stand, still covered, for 3–5 minutes at the end of the time. Fluff up the grains with a fork before serving.

Frozen Cooked Rice Turn the frozen rice into a dish, separating the grains if necessary. Add 1 tablespoon water, cover the dish and cook on full. Stir halfway through, then toss with pepper and melted butter before serving.

225–350g/8–12oz	4–6 minutes
450–575g/1–1¼lb	7–10 minutes

> **Note** *100g/4oz rice yields about 350g/12oz when cooked and 225g/8oz about 575g–675g/ 1¼–1½lb.*

RICE PUDDING

This can be cooked in the microwave but it is essential to use a deep dish or bowl as the milk boils up and unless there is plenty of space in the dish it will spill over, making an unpleasant mess. When the rice and milk are in the dish it should be about a quarter full - or less! A mixing bowl is suitable (use a plate as a lid) or a very deep casserole is ideal (one that just fits into the height of the average microwave). The shape of the dish does affect the cooking time and if the lid fits well, then less moisture escapes and this can also slightly lengthen the cooking time. Try the recipe and decide whether you think it is worth cooking in the microwave – if you are concerned that the dish is not deep enough then stay near to make sure the milk does not boil over. Next time you will know which dish to use and then you will be able to let the pudding cook without standing nearby to watch it.

Traditional Rice Pudding Place 50g/2oz round-grain rice in a deep dish (use a mixing bowl with a plate for a cover) and add 50g/2oz sugar. Stir in 600ml/1 pint milk, a knob of butter, a strip of lemon rind and a little grated nutmeg, then cook on full for 7–9 minutes, until the milk boils. Stir well, cover and cook for a further 35–40 minutes on low, stirring twice, until the rice is cooked. Leave to stand for 5 minutes before serving.

Creamed Rice Pudding This is truly delicious, fail-safe and very speedy – but it's not cheap! Cook 50g/2oz round-grain rice with 50g/2oz sugar and 600ml/1 pint water on full for 20–25 minutes in a covered dish. At the end of the cooking time the rice should be thick and very sticky. Immediately stir in 300ml/½ pint cream (single or double) and heat for 30–60 seconds on full before serving. This is also very good cooled and chilled, with fresh fruit, a dash of sherry or rum added or sprinkled with toasted flaked almonds.

SAGO

It is essential to use a deep casserole or bowl for this as the milk boils up during cooking and it may spill over. Place 50g/2oz sago in a large dish or bowl. Add 25g/1oz sugar and stir in 600ml/1 pint milk. Cook on full for 13–16 minutes, stirring twice, until the grain is cooked and the pudding thickened.

SALMON

This fish requires very little cooking and the

microwave is useful for the purpose.

Defrosting Salmon Steaks Place the steaks as far apart as possible on a dish and cover with absorbent kitchen paper. Use defrost setting and turn the steaks halfway through the time. Allow 4–6 minutes per 450g/1lb.

Cooking a Whole Salmon A whole fish weighing up to 2.25kg/5lb can be cooked successfully in the microwave. The gutted fish should be scaled and all fins trimmed off. When trimming off the fins make sure that you slit the skin of the fish in two or three places to prevent it from bursting during cooking. Place 1 or 2 bay leaves in the body cavity and curl the fish into a large flan dish. Cover the fish with special microwave film, wrapping two layers over the dish to keep the salmon firmly in place. Cook on full for 2–3 minutes per 450g/1lb. A 2.25kg/5lb fish will need about 10–15 minutes. Leave the salmon to stand for 5 minutes before checking that it is cooked by piercing the flesh at the thickest point. The cooked salmon should be moist and the flesh should flake easily.

Cooking Salmon Steaks Tuck the flaps of flesh neatly into the middle of the steaks and keep them in place with wooden cocktail sticks. Arrange the steaks in a dish, placing them as far apart as possible, with the thicker sides towards the edge of the dish and the flaps in the middle. Dot with butter and sprinkle with 1 tablespoon water. Cover and cook on full for 4–5 minutes per 450g/1lb. Turn the steaks halfway through cooking.

SALT

Getting used to microwave cooking means adjusting traditional ideas about adding salt to food. When cooking food which is not in any sauce, then do not add salt before cooking. This applies to fish, poultry and meat, vegetables and eggs; when salt is sprinkled over dry food it tends to result in dried patches when cooked. Sauces, soups, rice, pasta and casserole-style dishes can all be salted before cooking.

SAUCES
See Béchamel Sauce, page 20; Cheese Sauce, page 20; Onion Sauce, page 20 etc.

There are definite advantages to cooking sauces in the microwave – there is no hot saucepan base to cause sticking and burning; there is less likelihood of the sauce being lumpy since it does not stick, the cooking time is reduced and there is less washing up.

For success, use a large jug or basin to cook sauces as this allows plenty of room for whisking the liquid during cooking. And the rule is to whisk not stir most sauces as this distributes the cooked flour or other thickenings more evenly and makes the sauce smooth.

Delicate sauces are less likely to go wrong in the microwave but exercise the same care as you would with conventional cooking and do stand nearby, making sure the sauce does not begin to overcook, boil or curdle.

Remember that sauces can be made in advance and reheated in the microwave just before they are served. A sauceboat which is suitable for microwave cooking is useful as the sauce can be heated in it.

SAUSAGES
Without a browning dish it is not possible to cook sausages successfully in the microwave. They do not brown and the skin will not become crisp. Skinless sausages can be cut up and cooked as part of a full-

flavoured casserole to give results which are just acceptable, but cooked on their own they taste like steamed sausages.

However, frozen sausages can be successfully defrosted in the microwave. Unwrap and place them on absorbent kitchen paper on a plate. If they are separate, then place the sausages as far apart as possible. Use defrost setting and separate sausages in a block as soon as possible during cooking.

225g/8oz – 3–5 minutes	
450g/1lb – 5–7 minutes	

Pat them dry and cook under a hot grill.

SCALLOPS

These are very delicate and they become tough when overcooked. They can be poached in a little liquid or sauce with great success in the microwave. Stir the scallops once or twice during cooking to ensure that any at the edge of the dish are not overcooked.

Defrosting Scallops Place them as far apart as possible on absorbent kitchen paper on a plate. Cover with more paper and use defrost setting. Check the scallops halfway through the time and turn or rearrange them. They should still be icy when ready for cooking.

4 scallops – 3–5 minutes	
8 scallops – 5–8 minutes	

Poached Scallops Finely chop half a small onion and cook it with a knob of butter on full for 1–2 minutes. Stir in 1 tablespoon flour and 150ml/¼ pint dry white wine, light fish stock or dry cider. Add a bay leaf, a little seasoning and 8 scallops. The scallops can be cooked whole or halved, depending on their size. If you like, cut them into thick slices. Cover the dish and cook on full for 4–6 minutes, until the scallops are just firm and the sauce lightly thickened. The sauce can be enriched by adding 2 tablespoons double or soured cream. Serve the scallops in a ring of browned, piped mashed potatoes; in a crisp-baked bread case; on small, neat slices of toasted or fried bread; or they are good as a filling for pancakes. To serve them very simply, spoon the scallops into individual dishes and top with chopped parsley, then accompany with crusty bread.

SCONES
These cannot be cooked successfully in the microwave. They can be made to rise and set if an egg is added to the mixture but the result has an unpleasant 'raw' flavour.

SEMOLINA
See also Gnocchi, page 84.

This is excellent in the microwave and there is no danger of burning it on to the base of a hot saucepan. Heat 600ml/1 pint milk and 50g/2oz sugar in a large dish or bowl on full for 5 minutes, until hot but not boiling. Slowly whisk in 40g/1½oz semolina. Cook on full for a further 4–6 minutes, whisking halfway through cooking. The cooked semolina should be thick and smooth.

Serve semolina topped with jam, honey or stewed fruit. Alternatively, stir 100g/4oz plain chocolate (broken into squares) into the semolina. When the chocolate has melted top each portion of semolina with some whipped cream.

SHORTCRUST PASTRY
See Pastry, page 113, and Combination Microwave Cooking, page 50.

This does not cook well in the microwave.

SOUFFLÉS

These cannot be cooked in the microwave as they rely on traditional heating methods to form a crust which will hold the risen soufflé up. It is not possible to cook a good soufflé by combination microwave cooking.

SOUPS

A wide variety of soups can be cooked in the microwave. The rule to remember is that large quantities of liquid take some time to boil in the microwave, so the kettle is your microwave's best friend. When making soup, cook the main ingredients (vegetables, chicken etc) in a small amount of liquid until tender. Then add the remaining liquid, using boiling water from the kettle if possible, and continue cooking. If you add all the liquid at the beginning, then ingredients like potatoes, leeks or other vegetables will take a long time to become tender as the microwaves have to heat all the liquid first.

Leek and Potato Soup Place 1 chopped onion in a bowl or large dish with a knob of butter and cook on full for 3 minutes. Add 1kg/2lb diced potatoes and 2 sliced, large leeks. Mix in 150ml/¼ pint hot stock and cover. Cook on full for 14–16 minutes, or until the vegetables are tender. Add a further 450ml/¾ pint hot stock and cook on full for 5–7 minutes. Blend the soup in a liquidiser, season it to taste and heat for 2–5 minutes on full. Add a little single cream before serving.

SPAGHETTI

Unless you break the spaghetti into short pieces and cook it as for pasta shapes (see page 113) it is best to cook this pasta by traditional methods, curling it into a large pan of boiling salted water.

SPECIALIST COOKWARE

There is an enormous variety of specialist cookware available for use in the microwave. The best advice is to get used to microwave cooking before spending a fortune on cookware. Check all your ordinary dishes and decide which are suitable for microwave cooking, then buy just one or two new items. Once you have established exactly how you make the best use of the microwave, then you will know whether ring dishes and cake dishes, browning dishes and microwave roasting racks are going to be used in your kitchen.

The specialist cookware varies significantly in quality and some very light plastic utensils have a limited life. The rigid microwave ware that also withstands temperatures of up to 190–200C/375–400F in a conventional oven is designed to last and this is reflected in the price. A range of ovenproof glassware with a special non-stick coating is now available; this includes loaf dishes, flan dishes and round dishes, and is ideal for use in the microwave as well as the conventional oven.

Look out for new gadgets that are always appearing in the shops; for example it is now possible to buy a small sandwich or waffle toaster for use in the microwave, and a pressure cooker is available for tenderising meats (see page 126).

One point to remember is that specialist cookware is usually made of materials through which microwaves pass most easily, with the very minimum of absorption. This can mean that the food cooks quicker when placed in these specialist containers.

If you are in the process of equipping your kitchen, then it is certainly as well to consider microwave cooking and to look at the more expensive ranges of oven-to-table, microwave-proof ware, as it will provide the maximum flexibility.

SPINACH
Either fresh or frozen, this cooks well in the microwave.

Frozen Spinach Since frozen spinach is usually served hot, in cooked dishes, it can be defrosted quite successfully on full. Place blocks or free-flow chips of spinach in a large bowl or dish and cover. Break up the blocks frequently during defrosting and stir small chunks of frozen spinach several times. At the end of the time, mix the spinach thoroughly and allow it to stand for 5 minutes before draining off any excess liquid (if required). Allow 5–7 minutes per 450g/1lb on full. The vegetable should still be slightly icy.

Cooking Frozen Spinach Once defrosted, allow an extra 2–5 minutes per 450g/1lb on full, stirring once more, until the spinach is thoroughly heated.

Cooking Fresh Spinach Place the trimmed, wet leaves in a bowl or large roasting bag. Cover or close the bag with a microwave-proof tie. Cook on full, rearranging halfway through cooking. Allow 5–7 minutes per 450g/1lb. Drain well and use or serve as required.

SPONGE PUDDING
The microwave cooks sponge pudding in a fraction of the time taken to steam it and the result tastes just as good. Because the pudding rises rapidly the mixture should be cooked in a large basin.

Beat together 50g/2oz butter or margarine, 50g/2oz caster sugar, 50g/2oz self-raising flour, 1 egg and 2 tablespoons milk. The mixture should be really soft, light and pale. Place about 100g/4oz jam in the bottom of a well-greased 1.15 litre/2 pint basin and spoon the pudding mixture on top. Cook on full for 3 – 5 minutes, until the pudding is well risen and firm but still slightly sticky on top. Leave to stand for 5 minutes before turning out and serving with custard.

Vary the pudding by adding dried fruit or grated lemon rind. Marmalade or syrup can replace the jam.

STANDING TIME

This term is used a lot in microwave recipes, or sometimes it is suggested that the food should be 'left to rest'. When food is cooked by microwaves it does become very hot and this heat is not always evenly distributed throughout the food. The point of standing time is to let the very hot bits cool slightly and pass on their heat to the cooler areas. During standing time any small parts of food which are not quite cooked will often finish cooking by means of the heat which comes from a neighbouring hot area.

When large, dense pieces of food are cooked by microwaves, then it is essential to observe the standing times and to make sure that the food is kept in the hot dish, closely covered or wrapped in foil with the shiny side inwards, so that the maximum heat is kept in the food to finish off the cooking.

Often, with moist food or small amounts, the time taken to remove the dish from the microwave and to stir the contents is enough to cover the suggested standing time. So, adopt a sensible approach and always observe the suggested standing time but do take into consideration the time that you may well spend serving the food.

When defrosting food in the microwave standing times are very important. The food should be still quite icy when it comes out of the microwave and the standing time is essential to defrost the food further.

STERILISING JARS
It is possible to use the microwave to sterilise pots for preserving. Make sure that the pots are free of all metal, then half-fill them with boiling water from the kettle and put in the microwave. Cook on full for 2–5 minutes, or until the water has boiled for about 2 minutes. Drain and dry the pots, then fill.

> *If you sterilise the pots in advance, then cover each one with microwave-proof cling film and leave in the microwave, still filled with water. Heat briefly before emptying and drying them just before use.*

STIRRING
The reason for stirring food in the microwave is to move items from the outside of the dish, where the food receives most microwave energy, into the middle where it receives less. This ensures that the food cooks evenly.

Food is often stirred at the end of the cooking time, particularly sauced dishes, and this is to distribute the heat evenly. It is important to stir coffee or other drinks which are heated in the microwave before tasting them as you may sip from a hot spot and burn yourself.

STOCK
Fish Stock Place fish trimmings – heads, bones and skin – in a bowl or large dish. Add 225g/8oz inexpensive white fish, for example coley, and pour in 300ml/½ pint boiling water. Add a bay leaf, 2 parsley sprigs and 1 sliced onion. Cover and cook on full for 7–10 minutes, then leave to stand for 5

minutes. Add a further 300ml/½ pint boiling water, cover and cook on full for 5 minutes. Leave to stand for 5 minutes, then strain and use as required.

Chicken Stock Break up a chicken carcass and place in a bowl or deep dish. Alternatively use 1 chicken quarter. Add 1 sliced onion, 1 bay leaf, 1 sliced carrot and 2 parsley sprigs. Pour in 300ml/½ pint boiling water and cover the dish. Cook on full for 9–11 minutes, until the raw chicken, if used, is well cooked. Pour in a further 900ml/1½ pints boiling water and cover the dish. Cook for a further 10 minutes on full, then leave to stand for 5 minutes before straining the stock.

SUET PASTRY
See Dumplings, page 70.

This can be cooked successfully in the microwave. For the following recipe use 100g/4oz self-raising flour mixed with 50g/2oz suet and a pinch of salt. Bind with about 50ml/2fl oz cold water and press lightly together.

Roly-Poly Roll out the suet pastry to an oblong and spread the middle with filling. Fold the edges over, then roll up the pastry and place the roly-poly on a greased flan dish or in a roasting bag. Cover and cook on full for 5–8 minutes, until the pastry is risen and firm. Use a cooked savoury filling – chopped onion with cooked ham or bacon, tomatoes and mushrooms – or a sweet filling such as jam.

SWEDE
Peeled, cubed swede cooks well in the microwave. Place in a dish with 3 tablespoons water, cover and cook on full, stirring to rearrange the pieces halfway through cooking. Allow 12–15 minutes for 450g/1lb. The cooked swede should be evenly tender.

SWEET AND SOUR SAUCE

Roughly chop 1 onion and place it in a dish with 1 green pepper, cut in chunks, and 1 carrot, diced. Add 2 tablespoons oil, cover and cook on full for 5 minutes. Mix in 2 teaspoons cornflour, 2 tablespoons tomato ketchup, 2 tablespoons soy sauce, 1 tablespoon cider vinegar, 1 tablespoon sugar and 1 small can pineapple chunks in syrup. Make sure the sauce is smooth, then cook on full for 4–5 minutes, until boiling and thickened. Taste and sharpen with a little extra cider vinegar if you like.

SWEET CORN

Frozen Sweet Corn Place in a dish, cover and cook on full, stirring halfway through.

100g/4oz	– 2–4 minutes
225g/8oz	– 4–6 minutes
350g/12oz	– 6–7 minutes
450g/1lb	– 7–10 minutes

Canned Sweet Corn Empty the corn into a dish, cover and cook on full for 2–5 minutes, until hot. A large can will need stirring halfway through.

Sweet Corn Relish A good relish for burgers! Mix 1 chopped onion with 1 large crushed clove garlic, 1 diced green pepper and 2 diced carrots in a large dish or bowl. Cover and cook on full for 5 minutes. Mix 2 tablespoons water with 300ml/½ pint cider vinegar, 100g/4oz sugar, ½ teaspoon turmeric and 2 tablespoons prepared mustard. Add this to the vegetables, then cover and cook on full for a further 5–6 minutes. Add 350g/12oz frozen sweet corn and stir well. Cook for a further 12–15 minutes on full, stirring frequently, until thickened. Pot the relish and top with airtight lids.

SYRUP

Make syrup for fruit salad in the microwave. Mix 100g/4oz sugar with 250ml/8fl oz water and the pared rind of ½ lemon. Cook on full for 5–6 minutes, until the sugar has dissolved and the syrup is boiling. Stir well to make sure that the sugar has dissolved. Allow to cool, discard the lemon rind and use as required.

TEA

Use the microwave to heat a mug of water if you want to make a single cup of tea using a tea bag. When the water is boiling – about 1 minute 15 seconds on full – drop the tea bag into the cup. This saves boiling a kettle. Water can also be boiled in a jug to make two or more cups, allowing about 4–5 minutes for 300ml/½ pint and 6–8 minutes for 600ml/1 pint.

TEMPERATURE PROBE

Some microwave cookers have a temperature probe which plugs into the side of the oven. The probe is inserted into the food to register the internal temperature. The temperature at which the food will be cooked is entered into the controls on the oven and the probe will monitor the cooking progress. When the requested temperature is reached the microwave will automatically switch off. This can be useful for cooking joints of meat but it is not a feature which is enormously useful.

THERMOMETERS

Do not use ordinary thermometers in the microwave. Special meat thermometers are manufactured for use in the microwave and they are useful for determining when a joint is cooked.

TOASTED SANDWICHES

Among the many gadgets available you may well come across a sandwich toaster especially designed for use in a microwave oven.

Without a special toaster it is still possible to make bubbling hot sandwiches from slices of toast and a suitable filling. Toast the bread conventionally on both sides, then sandwich the slices together with cheese, ham, cooked meats or your favourite filling. Place the sandwich on a double thick piece of absorbent kitchen paper on a plate and cook on full until the filling is hot. The timing depends on the number of sandwiches and the type of filling – cheese melts quickly and becomes very hot, but it is very quick so stand close by and watch the food cooking. Allow between 30 seconds and 2 minutes, and cook up to two or three sandwiches at once. Do not cook a large batch as the timing is increased and this will result in inferior sandwiches. Better to cook them in two or more batches.

TOMATOES

Tomatoes heat rapidly in the microwave. Their skins should be slit (cut a cross in the top of each one) or they can be halved or quartered before heating. Season them with pepper and dot with butter if you like. Cook on full.

1–2 tomatoes – 30–60 seconds
3–4 tomatoes – 2–3 minutes

Tomatoes on Toast These make a good snack. Chop 4 spring onions and cook them in 50g/2oz butter on full for 1 minute. Add 8 quartered tomatoes (peel them first if you prefer) and some pepper. Cook on full for 5–7 minutes, stirring once, then add some chopped parsley and salt to taste. Serve on freshly made toast. For a half quantity allow about 2–3 minutes cooking time.

Stuffed Tomatoes Cut off lids and scoop the middles out of 4 large tomatoes (or beef tomatoes); drain them upside-down on absorbent kitchen paper. Melt 25g/1oz butter with 1 small crushed clove garlic on full for 45 seconds. Stir in 100g/4oz fresh bread-crumbs, some chopped fresh herbs, 50g/2oz chopped mushrooms and 25g/1oz chopped walnuts or pea-nuts. Season with pepper and divide between the tomatoes. Place as far apart as possible on a dish and dot with a little extra butter or sprinkle with grated Parmesan cheese. Cook on full for 3–5 minutes.

Tomato Purée Use the microwave to cook tomatoes for making a fresh tomato purée. Quarter the tomatoes and place in a dish. Cover and cook on full until the tomatoes are mushy: 6–8 minutes for 450g/1lb; 10–12 minutes for 1kg/2lb. Leave to stand for 5 minutes, then press through a sieve.

Tomato Sauce Mix 1 finely chopped onion, 1 crushed clove garlic, 1 bay leaf, 1 chopped celery stick, 1 small chopped carrot and 2 tablespoons oil in a dish. Cover and cook on full for 5 minutes. Stir in 2 tablespoons flour, salt and pepper, 2 teaspoons sugar and 150ml/¼ pint boiling stock. Add 1 kg/2lb roughly chopped ripe tomatoes or two 400g/14oz cans chopped tomatoes. Cover and cook on full for 9–11 minutes, until the ingredients are cooked. Discard the bay leaf, blend the sauce in a liquidiser until smooth, then press through a sieve. Taste and adjust the seasoning, adding a little extra sugar if necessary.

TONGUE
Tongue requires long slow cooking and it cannot be cooked successfully in the microwave.

TOUCH CONTROLS
These afford greater accuracy than dial controls when timing very short periods. They are useful when selecting a 15 second cooking time, for example for warming cheese or bread rolls. However, when cooking for such a short period there is no great hardship attached to standing beside the microwave to monitor the progress closely.

TRIPE
This should be cooked by long, slow traditional methods.

TROUT
These fish cook well in the microwave to give full-flavoured, succulent results.
Defrosting Trout Unwrap the frozen fish and place in a dish. Cover and use defrost setting. Turn the trout at least once during defrosting and rearrange them if necessary. When ready the fish should still be lightly frozen in the body cavity. Leave to stand for 5 minutes, then rinse the body cavity under cold water and pat dry before cooking.

1 trout – 5–7 minutes	
2 trout – 8–10 minutes	
3 trout – 12–15 minutes	
4 trout – 15–20 minutes	

Cooking Trout The fish can be cooked with or without heads, as you prefer. Snip off the fins and make sure that the skin of the trout is pierced. Place a bay leaf in each body cavity and arrange the fish in a dish head to tail. Sprinkle with 2 tablespoons water, cover and cook on full. Turn and rearrange the trout halfway through cooking.

1 trout – 2–3 minutes	
2 trout – 4–6 minutes	
3 trout – 5–7 minutes	
4 trout – 8–10 minutes	

Check to see if the fish are cooked by piercing the thickest part of the flesh with the point of a knife. The flesh should be moist and still very slightly under cooked when removed from the microwave. By the time they are served the trout will have finished cooking. Pour over almonds browned in butter (see page 6) if you like.

> *Note If you do not have a dish suitable to hold four trout, and the fish are quite large, then cook them in two batches of two each. Cover the cooked fish with foil, shiny side inwards, while the second pair are cooking. This works quite successfully.*

TURKEY

A small whole turkey can be defrosted and cooked in the microwave. The result is good and best if the outside of the bird is browned under a grill or in a hot oven before serving.

Since the bird is of uneven shape, it is necessary to use foil to shield small protruding areas on the wings and legs, and possibly the top of the breast, to prevent them overcooking.

Defrosting Turkey Calculate the time on defrost setting at 5–7 minutes per 450g/1lb. Unwrap the bird and place it in a dish. Turn the turkey frequently during defrosting, shielding small areas with foil as necessary to prevent them from becoming hot and beginning to cook. Halfway through the calculated time leave the turkey to stand for 15 minutes. Drain away the liquid from defrosting and check to see if the giblets can be removed from the body cavity. Continue defrosting, then leave the turkey to stand for 20 minutes at the end of the time. The bird should still be slightly icy. Remove the giblets if they are still in the body and scald the cavity with boiling water.

Cooking Turkey Calculate the cooking time at 6–8 minutes per 450g/1lb on full, weighing the prepared bird with any stuffing. The bird should be neatly trussed. Place the turkey breast down in a dish and cover the dish; it will sit a bit lopsided but this does not matter. Use a roasting bag or microwave cling film if you do not have a suitable dish with a lid. Turn the turkey frequently during cooking, so that the whole area cooks through. Keep the breast meat down in the cooking juices for the majority of the time to keep the meat moist. Halfway through cooking leave the turkey to stand for 20 minutes, wrapping it in foil with the shiny side inwards. Remove the foil and continue cooking, ending with the breast uppermost. Season the skin with a little salt and baste it with cooking juices, then brown the bird under the grill or in a hot oven.

Cooking Turkey Drumsticks Calculate the cooking time at 5–7 minutes on full per 450g/1lb. These are not the ideal shape for microwave cooking and results are not as good as by conventional roasting. The thin end of the drumsticks may need shielding during cooking; if possible arrange the thin ends towards the middle of the dish, or push them close up to the thicker part of a neighbouring drumstick. Cook in a covered dish and turn once or twice during cooking.

TURNIPS

Small whole turnips cook well in the microwave. If they are large they should be halved or cut into evenly sized pieces. Place the vegetables in a dish and sprinkle with 3 tablespoons water. Cover and cook on full, stirring halfway through the time.

225g/8oz – 5–7 minutes	
450g/1lb – 9–11 minutes	

Leave, closely covered, for 5 minutes, then drain and toss in butter, adding a good grind of black pepper. The turnips are delicious coated in cheese sauce then browned under a hot grill.

TURNTABLE

The majority of microwaves have turntables as a standard feature; however there is no reason why an oven without a turntable should give inferior cooking results. A good quality oven without a turntable offers the advantage of extra space and the facility for using larger, oblong dishes that do not fit on to a round turntable. To an extent the price and manufacturer's reputation is a good guide when buying, and, of course, look out for the British Electrotechnical Approvals Board mark which indicates that the appliance has been tested and found to be manufactured to a satisfactory standard.

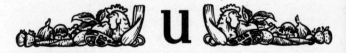

UTENSILS

Always avoid metals. Ovenproof glassware is useful and specialist cookware is made from materials that are ideally suited to microwave cooking. Before buying new equipment, look at your existing dishes and pick out casseroles and dishes that are not decorated with metal and able to withstand the temperatures reached by the cooked food. Baskets, wood and paper can be used for short heating times. Unglazed earthenware does absorb a certain amount of microwave energy (it becomes hot during cooking) but it can be used for cooking. The cooking time may be increased but the fact that the food cooks slightly slower can be an advantage.

> *Wooden spoons can be left in a bowl of food which is heated briefly in the microwave but the wood does absorb energy and it will become very hot if left in the dish for any length of time.*

VEAL

Tender cuts of veal can be cooked in the microwave but stewing veal should be cooked by conventional methods.

Defrosting Veal To defrost whole joints, follow the instructions for beef, see page 20. Escalopes, chops and steaks can be defrosted speedily – place on a dish, separating them if possible, and cover with absorbent kitchen paper. Cook on defrost setting, turning halfway through the time. Leave to stand for 10 minutes before cooking.

1 –	2–5 minutes
2 –	4–6 minutes
3 –	5–7 minutes
4 –	7–9 minutes

Cooking Veal Joints Calculate the cooking time for veal joints at 7–9 minutes per 450g/1lb on full and turn frequently during cooking. Leave to stand for 15–20 minutes at the end of the calculated time. Like other large cuts of meat, best results are really obtained by conventional roasting; however, the joint can be partly cooked by microwaves, then finished off in a conventional oven, or it can be virtually cooked through then browned very quickly in the oven or under the grill.

Cooking Veal Escalopes Tender escalopes of veal cook well in the microwave. For best results beat the escalopes until thin, then roll them up and cook in a sauce. The veal can be spread with herb butter or topped with a slice of ham before it is rolled. Secure the rolls with wooden cocktail sticks or string, then arrange in a dish. Add 300ml/½ pint hot stock, white wine, or a mixture of both. A bay leaf and other herbs can be added for flavour. Cover and cook on full, turning the veal rolls halfway through the time.

2 rolls – 3–4 minutes	
4 rolls – 5–7 minutes	

Remove the rolls then thicken the sauce with 2 tablespoons flour beaten with 25g/1oz butter. Whisk this into the liquid and cook on full for 2 minutes, or until boiling and thick. Add seasoning to taste and a little single cream if you like. Replace the veal, coat in sauce and heat for 30 seconds on full before serving if necessary.

Minced Veal This can be cooked in the same way as minced beef (see page 22). It makes good burgers or meatballs, and a meat sauce made with veal is a tasty filling for pancakes.

WARMING PLATES
To warm plates in the microwave, sprinkle each with a little water and stack them up. Place a mug half filled with water on top and cook on full for 2 minutes. The plates will be warmed and ready to be dried for serving the food.

Alternatively, use the plates as a cover for the cooking dish. Wipe the base of the plate which has been directly over the food before serving the meal.

WAVE GUIDE
This is the component which directs the microwaves from the magnetron, where they are produced, into the oven cavity. Once inside the oven cavity the waves are reflected off the walls and base so that they can be absorbed by the food which is in the middle of the oven.

WHITE SAUCE, SAVOURY
To make a plain, unflavoured, savoury white sauce, follow the instructions for Béchamel Sauce (see page 20), omitting the bay leaf and mace. The sauce can be flavoured after cooking or used as a base for other dishes.

WHITE SAUCE, SWEET
To make a plain, sweet white sauce, blend 2 tablespoons cornflour with 3 tablespoons sugar and a little milk taken from 600ml/1 pint. Gradually stir in the remaining milk, then heat the sauce on full for

6–8 minutes, or until boiling. Whisk the sauce two or three times during cooking to make sure it is smooth. Once it has boiled the sauce should be cooked for a further 30–60 seconds on full so that the cornflour is thoroughly cooked.

Brandy Sauce Add 3–4 tablespoons brandy to the sauce before serving.

Vanilla Sauce Add a little vanilla essence to taste.

Rum and Raisin Sauce Add 50g/2oz raisins to the sauce halfway through cooking and 4 tablespoons rum before serving.

WINE, MULLED
See page 128.

WINE SAUCE
A good savoury sauce for fish, poultry or meat, this can be used to coat ingredients before they are cooked in the microwave or it can be poured over cooked food.

Place a finely chopped small onion in a dish with 25g/1oz butter. Cook on full for 3 minutes, then stir in 2 tablespoons flour and add 300ml/½ pint white or red wine. Add a bay leaf and 2 tablespoons chopped parsley, then stir in 150ml/¼ pint water or stock. Red wine sauce can also be flavoured with a little tomato purée. Cook on full for 7–10 minutes, whisking two or three times until the sauce has boiled and thickened and the ingredients have given up their flavour. If the sauce is to be used as a base for cooking raw ingredients, then it should be cooked for about half this time – it will continue to cook when the food is added.

White wine sauce can be enriched by adding a little single or double cream. Discard the bay leaf before serving.

YOGURT
A note about using yogurt in cooking. Yogurt does curdle when it is overheated and this is true of the microwave as well as for conventional methods. Always add yogurt at the end of cooking so it is heated for the minimum time to prevent curdling. In most cases the heat of the cooked ingredients is enough to warm the yogurt and only seconds should be allowed to increase the temperature.

YORKSHIRE PUDDING
This cannot be cooked in the microwave; however it does cook successfully in a combination microwave oven (see page 50).

ZABAGLIONE
This creamy foam of eggs and sweet white wine can be cooked very easily in the microwave to make a superb dessert with little risk of curdling. Whisk 4 egg yolks with 25g/1oz caster sugar and 1 tablespoon grated lemon rind until the yolks are pale and creamy. Pour 150ml/¼ pint Marsala or other sweet white wine into a jug and heat on full for 1 minute, until hot but not boiling. Whisking continuously, pour the wine slowly into the yolks, then continue whisking until the mixture is frothy. Cook on full for 30 seconds and whisk again; continue cooking for a further 1–2 minutes, whisking every 30 seconds, until the zabaglione is slightly thickened and very foamy. Take care not to overcook the mixture or it will curdle. Pour into warmed glasses and serve with sponge fingers.

RECIPE INDEX

THE FAMILY MATTERS SERIES

Anniversary Celebrations 0 7063 6636 0
Baby's First Year 0 7063 6778 2
Baby's Names and Star Signs 0 7063 6801 0
Baby's Names 0 7063 6542 9
Card and Conjuring Tricks 0 7063 6811 8
Card Games 0 7063 6635 2
Card Games for One 0 7063 6747 2
Charades and Party Games 0 7063 6637 9
Children's Party Games 0 7063 6611 5
Dreams and Their Meanings 0 7063 6802 9
How to be the Best Man 0 7063 6748 0
Microwave Tips and Timings 0 7063 6812 6
Modern Etiquette 0 7063 6641 7
Travel Games 0 7063 6643 3
Wedding Etiquette 0 7063 6538 0
Wedding Speeches and Toasts 0 7063 6642 5